SPLITTING
WOOD
TO
SPLITTING
ATOMS

Memoir of an Opportunist
Driven by Purpose and
Sustained by Faith

Arthur A. Pasanen, M.S.E., P.Eng

FROM SPLITTING WOOD TO SPLITTING ATOMS

Scriptures taken from the Holy Bible, New International Version®, NIV®. Copyright © 1973, 1978, 1984, 2011 by Biblica, Inc.™ Used by permission of Zondervan. All rights reserved worldwide. www.zondervan.com The "NIV" and "New International Version" are trademarks registered in the United States Patent and Trademark Office by Biblica, Inc.™

Printed in Canada

Print ISBN: 978-1-4866-2135-4
eBook ISBN: 978-1-4866-2136-1

Word Alive Press
119 De Baets Street, Winnipeg, MB R2J 3R9
www.wordalivepress.ca

Cataloguing in Publication may be obtained through Library and Archives Canada

To my wife, Helen.

CONTENTS

ACKNOWLEDGEMENTS

I was smitten with Helen the moment I first looked into those beautiful blue eyes after crashing carts with her in the former A&P store in Deep River, Ontario. That has not abated one iota in the fifty-eight years of our journey together.

As I have reflected on those many years in writing these memoirs, I have realized how much I've taken for granted the awesome blessing it has been to me that God brought us together as one in holy matrimony. Helen's positive can-do attitude toward life, strong work ethic, and spiritual giftings have played a huge role in whatever success I have had, as well as in my spiritual maturity.

She is my partner, best friend, spiritual counsellor, and excellent (virtuous) wife as defined in Proverbs 31. Translating that description into the context of modern culture shows that Helen fits it to a T!

I am grateful for her assistance with producing this book, including all the typing. I'm also thankful for helpful comments from Liisa and Peter Farugia's review of it.

ACKNOWLEDGEMENTS

PREFACE

Art is one of many Canadian scientists who has spent more than thirty years in the Canadian nuclear industry. Like the unknown soldier, often their essential contributions and battles to reach solutions go unnoticed. They are behind-the-scenes superheroes of hope.

Having been his wife for fifty-eight years, I can truly say that he had a very rewarding career in a most difficult field that required precise and perfect solutions since power, the great power from atoms being split, needs to be controlled.

The vastness of knowledge and wisdom revealed through the sciences is being studied around the world. This small area of science called applied nuclear reactor physics provided much insight for Art. Many people, both men and women, provided him with supportive working conditions that promoted in him an eagerness to learn, turning his career into a very positive experience. He is truly grateful to have had the experience.

This book is the story of a boy born and raised in Bruce Mines, a small town in northern Ontario. He was born near the end of the Great Depression when economic conditions were dire. In order to live, he needed a blood transfusion with his mother a few days after birth. He survived and is, at eighty-five year of age, at last publishing his autobiography.

Only by the providence of God working through a relative was he able to work his way through an American university, earning a Master of Engineering (specifically, nuclear engineering) at the age of twenty-two. He went on to play an important role in the development of the Canadian nuclear energy program.

The example set by his parents and siblings was used by God to instill in him a positive work ethic and strength of character to face the many challenges ahead. This book tracks Art's life through his childhood in Bruce Mines, his education in Ann Arbor, Michigan, his marriage to his soulmate Helen, his work in the Canadian nuclear industry, and his vocation after retirement.

Over the years of our marriage, when Art shared events from his past I asked him to write them down. After accumulating a number of these stories, we began thinking that they would be of interest to our grandchildren. He and I discussed how they should be compiled. Having published a number of books, I encouraged Art to work with me in weaving them into a biography. His knowledge and experiences will be of great encouragement to those in high school who may be considering careers in the sciences or engineering, particularly in the fascinating arena of nuclear energy.

From the Holy Scriptures we are encouraged not to despise small beginnings. Art's story, like many others, demonstrates that the conditions under which we come into the world can be a springboard to success rather than a platform for complacency. A strong work ethic can strengthen one's character. Requiring children at an early age to be part of the solution in dealing with adversity generally builds in them positive virtues. Of course, one must also determine to seize opportunities when they are presented and become committed to do the work needed to overcome challenges. Persistence and strength are needed to run the race to the finish line.

Art believes the opportunities presented to him were orchestrated by God working through many kind and caring individuals from whom he received support, without which his achievements would not have been realized. The correlation of the time of Art's birth with the dawn of the nuclear energy age suggests that his life took the track he was destined for.

—Helen S. Pasanen

INTRODUCTION

Before the discovery that atoms of uranium could be divided or split into two smaller atoms to produce energy, mankind's sources of energy were limited to chemical combustion at the molecular level, gravity-driven potential energy, energy from the sun, and electricity.

It took thirty-five years of work by experimental physicists to discover that atoms consist of three types of particles. The electron was discovered by J.J. Thompson in 1897, the proton by Ernest Rutherford in 1920, and the neutron by Sir James Chadwick in 1932. The latter received a Nobel Prize for it in 1935, the year I was born.

The study of the neutron is imperative in understanding atomic physics. The beginning of the twentieth century had seen a lot of development in the field of atomic physics. Early in the century, Ernest Rutherford published a model of the atom of an element. He considered positively charged protons and negatively charged electrons to be packed inside a central nucleus, but his theory posed several contradictions in many studies. Hence through a series of experiments a third neutral particle, having a mass close to the proton, was discovered by James Chadwick in 1932. It was called a neutron.

The discovery of the neutron was an important milestone in the field of atomic physics. It gave scientists and researchers access to new tools for further experimentation in this field. Initially, alpha particles were used for scattering experiments, but this posed a problem if the nuclei were those of helium. The coulomb repulsive force barred any experimentation. The neutron, with its net neutral charge, did not have to overcome this force and thus facilitated several experiments which further opened new avenues in the field of atomic physics.

Nuclear fission was discovered experimentally in 1938 by physicists Lise Meitner and Otto Robert Frisch and chemist Otto Hahn Strassman. They found that when uranium was exposed to free neutrons, atoms of barium were found in the uranium. Further investigation by these scientists and others to explain this strange result made it clear that neutrons had somehow caused uranium atoms to divide into two atoms whose proton numbers added up to the total of the original uranium atom.

However, one of the neutrons in the original uranium atom was missing from the two products of the division (fission). This indicated that the fission had resulted in a conversion of mass to energy, because high-energy electromagnetic energy, called gamma rays, were also observed.

Amazingly, uranium mining has produced evidence that nuclear fission occurred naturally a very long time ago. This evidence was discovered forty-four years after it was found experimentally.

In 1972, the discovery occurred in the area of Gabon in western Africa, to the delight of many nuclear enthusiasts. Studies of the uranium located in this part of the world revealed interesting findings when analysis was taken of isotope ratios. These findings could only be explained by assuming that nuclear fission had occurred. Scientists were able to predict that the energy produced by these natural fission reactors was very low in comparison to today's manmade nuclear reactors. It was thought that these ancient fissions produced enough energy to put out one hundred kilowatts, enough to light up a thousand one-hundred-watt lightbulbs. Today's commercial nuclear reactors can produce enough to power about ten million lightbulbs!

Extensive research by scientists has revealed that there were at least seventeen natural fission reactors operating millions of years ago on Earth, according to conventional dating methods. Greed for the uranium found in Africa depleted most of these seventeen sites, however, and physicists advocated for the shutdown of the last known natural reactor uranium mine, Bangombe.

Studies conducted at these sites have provided very important insights relevant to nuclear power as well as waste management. It is interesting how scientists can unravel products, activities, and laws that existed long before humans were created. This is where the God factor comes into play; His wisdom and knowledge continues to be uncovered by curious, creative mathematicians and physicists.

The mass of an atom is proportional to the total number of neutrons and protons which are bound together to form the nucleus of the atom. Protons have a positive electrical charge that is balanced by an equal number of electrons orbiting the nucleus, making the atom electrically neutral. Electrons have very little mass. The neutron was so named because it carries no charge and so is electrically neutral. Many elements contain atoms that differ in the number of neutrons. They are called isotopes of the element and are identified by the mass number, which is the total number of neutrons and protons. The number of protons is called the atomic number.

Uranium in the natural state has two isotopes, U235 and U238. Both can be split by absorbing a free neutron, but the probability is very much higher for U235. However, only 0.72 percent of natural uranium is U235. The probability of fission is very dependent on the energy (speed) of the neutron. The neutrons released in fission have a high speed, so very few cause fissions.

The early experiments on nuclear fission of uranium indicated that in addition to dividing into a variety of pairs of atoms, two or three free neutrons were also released. This raised the exciting prospect of designing an energy system based on a self-sustaining chain of fission reactions in which matter is converted to energy according to Einstein's equation $E=MC^2$, where C is the speed of light.

This is a huge number. Some scientists predicted that the cost of fuel for such a system would be too small to measure. Because of the complexity of the nuclear process involved, it became clear that a major research program would have to be launched to prove the concept and develop the analytical methods needed to design a safe commercial system to produce electricity from nuclear energy.

Thirty-four years of my life was devoted to the nuclear energy program of Canada, mainly associated with the design and operation of CANDU power reactors.

Because my occupation as a nuclear engineer and reactor physicist represents only forty percent of my life, the majority of this memoir relates to my childhood, education, and post-retirement life. To assist the reader in better understanding why the memorable moments in my career with Atomic Energy of Canada were significant to me, I felt it necessary to explain the physics of nuclear reactors in some detail.

EARLY DAYS
IN BRUCE MINES

CHAPTER ONE

Bruce Mines, Ontario is located on the North Channel of Lake Huron, about forty miles from Sault Ste. Marie. It is the site of the first copper mine in Canada and has the added distinction of having been incorporated in 1903 as the first town in northern Ontario.

My parents, Charles and Hulda Pasanen, married in 1928. The copper mine had closed permanently in 1921 and it is presumed that they came to Bruce Mines because of other work opportunities, such as forestry or quarrying. My mother's parents, Nestor and Maria Freeman,[1] also lived in the town; perhaps that was another reason for my parents settling in Bruce Mines.

Although my father was a Finnish carpenter who had emigrated to Canada with the skill to build log structures, there was little work in the town when I was growing up. My dad went away for most of the winter to work at lumber camps north of Sault Ste. Marie.

Our family wasn't aware of the hardships my father had to endure at those camps. My wife Helen and I later watched a documentary about them at the museum in Sudbury, which revealed

---

[1] It is sometimes spelled Friiman.

the horrible conditions the workers lived in. This left no doubt in my mind about the reason my father contracted TB (tuberculosis), which he eventually died from at the age of fifty-four in a sanatorium in Woodstock. I was in Grade Twelve at the time.

I lived the first seventeen years of my life in Bruce Mines in a two-storey frame house on a half-acre lot at the north edge of town. My father built a small barn out of logs while I was growing up so we could have a cow.

There was also a log sauna on the property which we heated every Saturday. The heat source was a huge stack of large stones from a local quarry, sitting atop a firebox in which wood was burned most of the day to heat the stones to a high temperature. Enough energy could be stored in these stones to permit several groups of people to enjoy the sauna one after the other.

Because there was no chimney, the windows were left open to let out the smoke. This meant that the walls were covered with soot. I recently read a book, *The Finnish Way*, from which I learned that this type of sauna is still used in a limited way in Finland. It's called a "smoke sauna."[2]

I usually bathed in the sauna with my two older brothers, Edwin Eden[3] and Reino Pasanen, and later on with my brother-in-law, Melrose Wonch. There were three benches beside the hot stones and we would compete to determine who could stay on the top bench the longest as more and more water was thrown onto the stones from a bucket. Being the youngest, I usually lost.

Edwin would often go out in the winter and roll in the snow to cool off after a sauna. He also helped support the family by finding outdoor work during the years when I was going to school.

---

[2]   Katja Pantzar, *The Finnish Way* (New York, NY: Tarcher Perigee Penguin Random House, 2018).

[3]   Edwin was my half-brother from my mother's first marriage. Her first husband died of typhoid fever.

The house my family lived in was heated by a large barrel-type woodstove in the living room with stove pipes that ran through the upstairs bedrooms before going to the chimney. There was no indoor plumbing. Our water source was a shallow well with a hand pump and the toilet was a small outhouse about a hundred feet from the house; the waste was composted behind it. I was old enough to remember when electricity was first connected to the house. Before that time, we used oil lamps and candles for light.

The food supply came mainly from vegetables grown on the property, as well as a plot of land to the north that was owned by Edwin. It was used to grow enough potatoes to last the winter in a cold cellar under the house. Enough root crops—beets, carrots, and onions—were also grown to last the winter. During the summer, we enjoyed various greens. I remember the staple meal being a mixture of potatoes, beets, onions, and sometimes carrots during the winter.

A milk cow provided enough milk for the family. Bread was baked in a large cookstove with a wood-burning firebox. Eggs and meat were obtained from local farmers when money was available. During my high school years, my older brothers and brother-in-law would hunt deer and moose in the fall for meat.

When I was quite young, I remember my mother giving me a bath in a large galvanized tub placed on the kitchen floor. Water was heated in a pail on the cookstove.

Looking back, I realize that my family was living at what many would consider to be poverty level, but I don't remember ever feeling hungry. It had to be a great challenge for my parents to raise a large family in a house with three small bedrooms with little outside income or government support.

In spite of the hardships, such as having to go to the outhouse when the temperature was -35°F—all we had to clean ourselves was the paper from an Eaton's catalogue—I recall it as having been a mainly happy childhood with little family conflict. I give thanks to the Lord God for having been raised by a mother who necessarily had to assume responsibility beyond her years. She had been the second oldest of seven siblings who were raised on a small farm in Kipling, Ontario. Her father had to work away from home a lot, so my mother had to assume many parenting responsibilities, especially when her mother was ill. For example, she was usually the one to milk the cow. This experience prepared her well to deal with the even greater challenge of raising her own family of eight. She proved Romans 5:3–5 to be true:

> we also glory in our sufferings, because we know that suffering produces perseverance; perseverance, character; and character, hope. And hope does not put us to shame, because God's love has been poured out into our hearts through the Holy Spirit, who has been given to us.

My mother demonstrated strong virtues of endurance and character all her life. Even after her children were grown, she faced many challenges. She was widowed when she was in her fifties.

During the time that my father was in the sanatorium, my sister Helen who was two years older than me, married a man with little income. He was skilled in several trades, but he couldn't find steady work. Because they couldn't afford to look for their own accommodations, they were given permission to clean out and modify our family's barn to live in, since it no longer housed a cow. They had five children over a short period, which had to be quite a challenge for my sister since their dwelling was so very small. My mother surely offered as much assistance as she was able, but she still had to parent a daughter of her own, Elma, who was five years younger than I was, as well as her last son, Albert, who was ten years younger than me.

I am also very thankful for having had a father who was so committed to supporting his family in all the difficulties that arose from living through the Great Depression in the 1930s. The horrible working conditions in the lumber camps also demanded great endurance and strength of character.

Although I didn't develop a strong bond with my father because of the little time we shared together, there was evidence that Dad loved all his children. His first son Lawrence died at the age of twelve from a ruptured appendix. Although I was very young, I clearly remember how much my father cried when learning of the death.

Later, when my dad was in the sanatorium, all the children who were still at home had to be tested for TB. When my dad heard that I was at high risk of infection, he insisted that I not come to visit him in Woodstock, out of concern for my health.

Both of my parents were introverts who didn't communicate very much with their children at a deep spiritual level. I believe my mother had faith because of the influence of her own mother. If there had been a Lutheran Church in Bruce Mines, maybe we would have been involved. Many Finnish people consider themselves to be Lutheran because that's the state church of Finland.

I was the only one of my family who attended Sunday School for a few years, at the United Church. I'm not sure if my mother encouraged me to go or gave me permission when someone else invited me, but I remember being spiritually impacted by that experience. I feel it was part of God's plan for my life.

My grandparents lived in an older tar-paper-covered house that was smaller than ours. It was a one-storey house with an accessible attic where they had placed a bed for visitors. It was built on a small rocky lot close to the only beach in town. There was a hotel not far away that catered to tourists. My grandparents' house was about a half-hour walk through the bush from our house, but using town roads would make the trip at least twice as far.

A traumatic experience occurred when my mother heard that my grandfather was very ill. She sent me over to help my grandmother. She also contacted my Aunt Hilda, who was eight years younger than my mother. Aunt Hilda travelled a long distance to help her parents, and when she arrived I was in bed in the attic. She proceeded to join me.

In the middle of the night, I heard my Aunt Hilda call for me to come downstairs. I was so flustered that I tried putting my pants on by placing them over my head! By the time I got downstairs, my grandfather had died from a massive haemorrhage.

With my grandmother left alone, I had the responsibility of helping her as needed. At that time, I was the only male left in the household who was old enough to do this. So once a week after school I walked into town to shop for her and then return to her place along the town roads. She would have coffee ready for me and I'd receive Christian spiritual counsel from her.

This was another important step in my spiritual journey. I remember these visits as being very special. Afterward I would walk through the bush to get home, and in the winter it would be dark by the time I got there.

Throughout most of my high school years, I carried the male responsibility in the household, which mainly involved doing outdoor chores like splitting wood every day after school. Wood remained the energy source for heating and cooking, even after we had electricity supplied to the house.

Another memorable experience involved the house cat that kept the mice population under control. When it got sick, my mother asked me to take it into the bush and shoot it with the shotgun. Because of my inexperience, I had to shoot twice to kill the cat. It was one bloody and messy scene.

While weekdays were all work and no play, especially in the winter, I did have time to enjoy skiing with friends from school on the weekends. In the summer, we played softball, fished, and went swimming at the beach. I didn't get involved in hockey, because we couldn't afford the equipment.

My older brother Reino made skis for me out of hardwood. To bend the tips of the skis, he placed them in a tub of boiling water heated on the hot stones of the sauna. This softened the wood, allowing him to bend them into a frame. He didn't enjoy skiing himself.

Reino also built a treehouse with two rooms in a huge pine tree on county property far into the bush. This is where I spent time with my friend Bob Miller eating lunches during the school year. I often went skiing with Bob on weekends and remember insisting that we return to my house at 3:00 p.m. to enjoy coffee and the freshly baked Finnish sweet bread my mother had baked.[4]

When I was in Grade Twelve, my father passed away in the sanatorium early in the year. Aunt Hilda, who was living in Ann Arbor, Michigan at the time, came to Bruce Mines for the funeral. Since my mother had helped her in many ways when they were growing up in Kipling, Hilda had been thinking of ways to help our family.

Ann Arbor was home to the University of Michigan. Although Hilda and her husband George didn't have sufficient income to cover the expenses of a university student, Hilda invited me to go to Ann Arbor after graduating from Grade Twelve and apply for admission. They didn't have any children of their own,

---

[4]   This bread is often called *pulla* by the Finns.

and they assumed I would find enough work to cover most of my expenses except room and board.

At the time, students in Ontario only graduated after Grade Thirteen, but in the U.S. they graduated after Grade Twelve, so Hilda thought I could go to University of Michigan after the current year.

I knew I had no other prospects whatsoever of continuing my education beyond high school outside of a miracle like this. I felt both excited and frightened. I had no idea what courses I wanted to pursue and found the idea of going to university overwhelming. Hilda told me that I would need to think about it. I didn't need to come to a decision immediately.

As time went on, things fell into place and I ultimately decided to go for it.

Before I left, my grandmother moved to South Porcupine, Ontario to live with my Aunt Aili and her husband Ernest. Meanwhile, my sister Helen and her husband Mel were still living in the barn and would be able to support my mother when needed while I was gone.

When I presented the idea of attending university in Ann Arbor to my high school principal, Arthur Henderson, he offered to graduate me from Grade Twelve early, at Easter, because of my high grades and then spend the rest of the school year teaching me courses from the Grade Thirteen curriculum to better prepare me. This demanded a lot of extra work on his part.

Talk about encouragement! That cinched it for me. With that, I let Aunt Hilda know that I would be coming down in July of that year. This clearly showed the hand of God on my life.

THE QUANTUM
SHIFT IN SCHOOLING

CHAPTER TWO

In July 1952, at the age of seventeen, I found myself travelling from a town of five hundred people in northern Ontario to a city of more than fifty thousand in Ann Arbor, Michigan. I went with some trepidation, leaving all that was familiar to me and a family who loved me.

I had no idea of the challenges I would be facing. Aunt Hilda had shared very little about the University of Michigan, perhaps to avoid discouraging me. However, I was so thankful to know that I would not be facing these challenges alone, no matter what I encountered in the process. My aunt and uncle would give me any support they could.

As it turned out, Dr. Hinerman, a neighbour and good friend of Hilda and George's, lived across the street from them in this suburban part of Ann Arbor. He was a professor in the university's Department of Pathology. Because the first few weeks were so traumatic, I don't recall how much help I received from this professor in terms of applying for admission, but he likely told me exactly what I had to do. His assistance played a key role in my eventual success.

My introduction to the university blew me away. It was huge! I learned that there were about twenty-two thousand students registered. My graduating class in Bruce Mines had been six people!

Based on the documentation pertaining to my high school education, the admissions department set up an appointment for an interview with me. In the interview, I was told that because the university had no way to assess my academic qualifications I would have to complete a four-hour examination, the results of which would be used to decide my admissibility. My interviewer didn't give me any idea what the scope of the exam would be, and I had no opportunity to prepare for it.

After completing the challenging exam, I realized that I certainly hadn't aced it, as I was accustomed to doing in high school.

I was amazed and relieved to later meet with a professor who had reviewed the exam. He told me, "If you want to go into journalism, forget it. But if you choose to go into engineering, there's a good chance you will be accepted on the basis that you take three courses in the first semester without any credit toward your degree, to make up your deficiencies in mathematics and science."

"In that case, I would like to apply for admission to the engineering school," I replied.

This was a great leap of faith on my part. In Bruce Mines, I hadn't received any career counselling and, having grown up in isolation from the outside world—except for a few trips to see a movie with my Finnish friend Soini to Sault Ste Marie—I hadn't met or heard of a professional engineer. The only engineers I knew anything about were the people who drove trains.

The next challenge facing me was to choose the engineering discipline I wanted to train for, such as mechanical, electrical, civil, etc. I obtained a copy of the course curriculum for each of the disciplines, and after studying the courses I would have to take

I noticed there was one option that required more training in mathematics and physics than the others. It was called Engineering Mechanics. In Canada, the corresponding program is called Engineering Physics. I reasoned that taking this track would offer the most flexibility for my future career because of the extra training in math and physics. I also noted that the Engineering Mechanics curriculum required students to choose three courses specific to one of the other disciplines in the fourth year, giving them opportunity to change tracks at that point.

My application for admission to the Engineering Mechanics program was accepted on the basis that I would take three extra courses in addition to the what the curriculum required.

My next challenge was orientation week in September. At times I felt like a little country boy dropped into a big city. I felt totally disoriented. The university was divided into a north campus and a south campus, with an incredible number of different buildings in each. Imagine milling about in the midst of twenty-two thousand students, having never before been in a crowd of more than a dozen people at a time. It was stressful but absolutely necessary to prepare me for what was ahead. It took a whole week to get oriented!

Once registered, I had to face the funding challenge. I'd come to Ann Arbor with no money and my aunt and uncle didn't have the income to cover my expenses outside of room and board. Again, in hindsight it is clear that God's providence came into the picture.

Dr. Hinerman and his wife were very kind and unselfish people, and they came to my aid that first summer by hiring me to paint the siding on their house. I had no prior experience in painting, since my summer work in Bruce Mines had been focused on gardening, splitting wood, and helping my brother Reino cut pulpwood. I'd also worked at a farm where my best friend

Soini lived. I did okay by painting the house, except for spilling part of a gallon of paint on the asphalt shingles. I had to use a lot of paint thinner to clean up the mess.

Despite that, the Hinermans gracefully hired me later to sand and varnish a long hallway in their house while they were away on vacation. They rented a large belt sander but weren't able to explain how to use it. My Uncle George hadn't used one either, so he couldn't offer any guidance.

I was able to sand off the old finish on the boards very well and thought the floor looked nice and smooth. To my chagrin, when I applied the varnish the floor looked wavy! When the Hinermans returned, I apologized profusely.

"That's okay, Art," Mrs. Hinerman simply said. "We will put a runner on it and it will look fine."

During my first year at university, Dr. Hinerman, by some miracle was able to convince the head of the Department of Pathology to hire me to work in a laboratory, processing tissues. It was a part-time position which enabled me to work all year-round. I was even given a two-week paid vacation! I worked from 7:00 p.m. to 11:00 p.m. each weekday. It was an ideal job for a student, as the actual working time varied from day to day depending on the number of tissues received. At times I only had to work one hour out of four, giving me three hours to do homework.

On top of that, Dr. Weller, the head of the department, hired me to work most weekends as a handyman. He was an avid flower gardener, so I learned a lot about horticulture from him. Dr. Weller had a wall on two sides of his property made with natural stone and mortar. I learned how to repair it. His wife also had me do housework and even drive her on errands in their Buick!

Because of the grace shown by these professors, I was able to cover all my university expenses and give a small amount back to my aunt and uncle to cover the cost of food.

At the beginning of my first year, I had to make another very important decision. Conscription was in place at that time and American students were strongly advised to enroll in an officer training program for one of the branches of the military. This would be taken in parallel with their university program. If they chose not to do this and were conscripted into the military after graduation, they would serve initially at the same level as a high school graduate. Consequently, they wouldn't be able to use their education in their military work, which they would if they were conscripted as officer.

If I chose not to enroll in the officer training program, I would therefore be committing myself to find work back in Canada. I decided to forego work opportunities in the U.S.

Another experience I had while at the university proved the old adage that says "no pain, no gain." Growing up in Bruce Mines, I hadn't had access to dental care, so my teeth were in bad shape. Thankfully, the university's dental school had a program through which students could perform dental work on other students as part of their training. Of course, they were under supervision. One of my molars needed a gold crown, and the process involved fitting a copper tube over the tooth. The tube would then be filled with a hot plastic liquid that would solidify when cooled with cold water. The procedure was painful, with the tooth being exposed to both the hot and then the cold. It wouldn't have been too bad if it had been done only once, but the student, being inexperienced, had to repeat it three or four times before the resulting mould was acceptable to the instructor.

Sixty-five years later, I still have that gold crown in my mouth. Dentists ask me, "Who put in that gold crown?" I only had to pay for the cost of materials. When I die, my family will stand to earn a huge profit should they ask that the gold be saved! More blessings from God.

At the end of the third year, I had to choose three courses from one of the other engineering disciplines to specialize in. I became aware of a new discipline called Nuclear Engineering, marking the start of the development of commercial power stations that used energy from nuclear fission of uranium to produce electricity. The more I learned about it, the more convinced I became that this was the field for me to pursue.

After discussing it with university officials, they strongly encouraged me to go on to the School of Graduate Studies in the Master of Science in the Engineering Program (Nuclear Engineering). Upon agreeing to this, I was allowed to take three courses in the nuclear engineering discipline in my fourth year.

I received my Bachelor of Science in Engineering (Engineering Mechanics) on June 16, 1956. One of my professors pointed out that many of the courses I had completed were also part of the curriculum for the Bachelor of Science in Engineering (Mathematics). Therefore, by taking a few more math courses in summer school, I also qualified for the Mathematics degree. I received that degree on August 18, 1956. I then received my Master's in Nuclear Engineering on August 19, 1957.

I was able to earn these three degrees in five years because, with God's help, I basically attended school nonstop. I took courses every summer to hold my job, but one summer I was able to travel back to Bruce Mines during my two-week vacation. I spent it repainting our house on the outside, because it was sorely needed.

I was encouraged by my professors to carry on for a PhD, but the demands of such a program were too daunting for me to consider. I wanted to find work so I could help my family financially.

THE
JOB QUEST

CHAPTER THREE

During my year in graduate school, I sought information from the university library about what was happening in Canada pertaining to nuclear energy. I was aided by the fact that one of my assignments was to conduct research into published literature about nuclear energy developments around the world.

I found a report from Atomic Energy of Canada providing detailed information on the NRU Research Reactor being installed at the Chalk River Nuclear Laboratories (CRNL), near Pembroke, Ontario. I'd had no idea that the Canadian nuclear energy program was being launched there along the Ottawa River when I was just nine years old.

In the late 1960s, I learned that the area around my hometown, Bruce Mines, was one of many sites toured in 1944 by a team scouting for possible locations for a nuclear research centre. I'm sure the townspeople were unaware of it, because it was a secret project in the beginning. This was to be the first nuclear reactor in the world outside the U.S.[5]

Since CRNL was the National Nuclear Centre for Canada, it appeared to be the only option I had for finding work. Consequently, I submitted a resume to their Human Resources Department. Of course, I was fully aware of the fact that the nuclear energy program in the U.S. was significantly more advanced than in Canada.

In the United States, the first electricity to be produced by nuclear fission occurred on December 20, 1951 in the experimental breeder reactor. This was a demonstration that it could be done, but the reactor wasn't connected to a grid. The first power reactor to be connected to a grid was started up in April 1957. It was the SM-1 reactor in Virginia.

A year after my graduation, the first fully commercial nuclear power station in the U.S. started up. The American nuclear power program was projected to grow rapidly to a total of a thousand reactors. As a result, there was a very high demand for nuclear engineers in the U.S. when I graduated. At least twenty-five jobs were advertised at the University of Michigan. This presented a strong temptation for me to work in the U.S. and take my chances on being drafted into the military at the lowest rank, but I resisted this possibility.

Again, the hand of providence was upon me, because at the time that my application was received at Chalk River, the NRU research reactor construction had been completed and the commissioning program was underway. This was by far the most powerful research reactor in the world. The Mechanical

---

[5]   The first human-made self-sustaining nuclear chain reaction had occurred under the viewing stands of the original Stagg Field; it was called Chicago Pile-1 (CP-1). The word "pile" was used because it was classified as a secret operation, just as it was in the early days of the Canadian program.

Engineering department was the first to respond to my application, so I received an offer, which I accepted.

Before I knew it, I found myself at CRNL. I was given a detailed tour of the facility, which was referred to by the locals as "the plant." I met my supervisor, who explained what I would be doing and set a start time. The tour guide was able to take me through the NRU reactor since it wasn't operating yet. I was absolutely awestruck by it.

When I arrived for duty on September 9, 1957, I was pleasantly surprised to learn that I would not be working in the Mechanical Engineering department. Instead I was directed to the NRU building to meet with the operations manager, Gib James. Apparently, Gib hadn't become aware of my application until the first day I was there. I learned from Gib that he, too, was an engineering graduate of the University of Michigan. Because of my Master's in Nuclear Engineering and my specialization in math and physics, Gib thought I would be an asset in the Reactor Physics Section of the NRU Reactor Operations Branch.

I am thankful that my first two supervisors were talented and gifted professionals who mentored me. The first was Dr. John Hilborn, who went on to invent self-powered instrumentation to be inserted in the reactor core to measure the density of neutrons, which is an indication of the power level at the location of the detector. He also invented a small experimental reactor called Slowpoke which was so inherently safe that it could be installed at university campuses for students to use to perform experiments as part of their training in nuclear science. A number of universities in Canada and other countries have installed these reactors.

John joined AECL in 1954, having earned a PhD in Nuclear Physics from McGill University, and worked as a reactor physicist from 1954 to 1991. He was responsible for planning and supervising the low-power commissioning of the NRU reactor, which started up shortly after I began working at NRU. I didn't participate in the start-up program, but the training I received from John proved valuable for responsibilities I carried later in my career.

John was also responsible for the low-power commissioning program of the NPD (Nuclear Power Demonstration) reactor which started up on June 4, 1962. NPD was located on the Ottawa River, three kilometres east of Rolphton and about twenty kilometres from Chalk River. NPD supplied the Ontario power grid with the first nuclear-generated electricity in Canada. It only produced twenty megawatts of electricity and was never intended to be a commercial-scale reactor, but rather a working system to test the feasibility of the CANDU concept, which I ended up working on for the majority of my career. It also served as a training centre for nuclear plant operators until 1987 when it was closed.

Since the reactors at Chalk River represented new technology, worldwide pioneers like John Hilborn had to invent much of instrumentation required for the safe operation of its reactors. The same was true of the equipment used by scientists conducting experiments involving the interaction of neutrons with matter. Dr. Bertrand Brockhouse received a Nobel Prize for his pioneering work in neutron spectroscopy during the period from 1950 to 1962. I had the privilege of working with him in setting up the reactor conditions for his experiments.

John Hilborn provided excellent on-the-job training for me in reactor physics, which helped me navigate the rather steep learning curve necessary to equip me for my career. He put in extra effort to help me. In one case, we were working on a problem that didn't get resolved by the time the last bus was scheduled to leave the plant for Deep River, where we lived. I was checking my watch and finally had to tell John that I had to leave to catch the bus.

"Don't worry, Art," John replied. "I took my car to work today."

After finishing the discussion, we walked to the parking lot, which by this time was mostly empty. John looked around, couldn't find his car, and then embarrassingly declared, "I guess I didn't drive in after all!"

Fortunately, after waiting for a while we were picked up by someone else who had worked overtime.

John was awarded the Order of Canada on December 6, 2017 for his pioneering contribution to Canada's burgeoning nuclear industry, which is a testimony to his qualifications. He moved on in 1959 to greater things, probably associated with the core physics analysis for the NPD power reactor, and was succeeded as the head of the Reactor Physics Section by Elgin Horton.

Elgin didn't have the postgraduate education in nuclear physics like John, but he also helped me move up the learning curve. After a year or two, he seized an opportunity to join Ontario Hydro's rapidly growing power reactor program. Elgin's demonstrated leadership ability resulted in him being promoted to management roles. He was ultimately named Vice President of Nuclear Operations and Chief Nuclear Officer for Ontario Hydro.

When Elgin left, I was promoted to section head. In that capacity, I was responsible for the physics analysis related to the operation of the reactor. In 1962, it was decided that the needs of the experimental nuclear physicists and the demand for radioisotope production could be more efficiently met by changing the fuel in the reactor from natural uranium to one in which the U235 content had been increased to nineteen percent. I was assigned the task of preparing a report for the operations manager detailing the design of the new fuel and the associated physics characteristics.

The NRU research reactor was the most powerful reactor in the world built for research purposes. It was ten times more powerful than NRX, which was the first high-power research reactor built at CRNL. It had been in operation for several years when I joined AECL. The power level and size of NRU blew away the professors at the University of Michigan who had taught me. In fact, when my professor read the report I submitted on the NRU design, he told me that it wasn't possible for a Canadian research reactor to be that powerful.

Radioisotopes are produced in a special location in the core of the reactor. Natural elements, when placed in the reactor, absorb neutrons, resulting in a radioactive isotope. Radioactive isotopes from the NRU reactor were used in all kinds of medical procedures.

For example, radioactive tracers for nuclear stress tests could be used to see if a person had blocked arteries. These tracers were produced from molybdenum, a hard, grey metallic element used in steel and other alloys. Cobalt, when exposed to neutrons, becomes radioactive cobalt-60. This is used to treat cancer patients, extending their lives by many years.

Radioactive cobalt from NRU was also used to sterilize medical tools, equipment, and supplies like PPE (personal protective equipment). It is now being produced at the Pickering and Bruce Power Reactor facilities in Ontario.

The following summary of the importance of radioisotope production in reactors was given in *The Mississauga News* on August 25, 2007:

> Nuclear energy and saving lives—it's not an association that many people readily make.

But Atomic Energy Canada Ltd. (AECL) is in the business of helping to save lives, some 76,000 each day, worldwide.

In addition to being the builder of the world-renowned CANDU reactors, AECL is the world's biggest producer of medical isotopes: enough to treat or diagnose cancer, heart disease and other illnesses in 25 million people globally each year.

The isotopes are produced in a National Research Universal (NRU) reactor and then further processed before the final product is delivered to hospitals. The NRU recently broke a record for isotope production, allowing for more than a million additional diagnostic scans for patients.

In Canada alone, about one million nuclear medicine procedures are performed yearly using the isotopes. Approximately 90 per cent of the procedures require Molybdenum-99 from NRU.

The NRU reactor was developed in 1957, when it was hailed as a landmark achievement in Canadian science and technology. To mark its 50th anniversary, a giant barbecue was held Wednesday at AECL's sprawling Sheridan Park complex in Mississauga.

"The NRU had a special purpose behind it when it was first built — to save lives," said Ken Petrunik, AECL's Chief Operating Officer, noting it was the largest reactor at the time.

A medical isotope is a very small quantity of radioactive substance used in the imaging and treatment of disease. New technologies enable medical isotopes to be delivered directly to the site of diseased cells. This is different from external beam radiation treatment where radiation is directed from outside of the body.[6]

The Reactor Physics Section was responsible for specifying the irradiation periods needed for radioisotope production. Determination of the refuelling schedule and calculation of the plutonium concentration in the spent fuel were also important parts of the work.

In reflecting back on this period in my life, I see God's providence. The engineer who acted as my guide on a detailed tour of the research centre, including the reactors, turned out to work in the Mechanical Engineering Department, whose manager had intended to hire me. Had I been hired into that branch, my career path would have been on engineering design rather than the physics analysis of nuclear reactions in a reactor core.

This sequence of events was part of God's plan, which I know because my tour guide was a Christian. He was led to befriend me and eventually invited me to work with him as a leader of a boys group called Tyros, a program for youth run by the Deep River Community Church. Naturally, I began attending church services regularly and even served on the board of elders for some time before leaving Deep River.

This was my introduction to the functioning of a Christian church and all part of the plan which eventually led me to form a personal relationship with Jesus and serve Him in various ways for the rest of my life.

---

[6]   Joseph Chin, "50 Years of Saving Lives," *Mississauga News*. August 25, 2007 (https://www.mississauga.com/news-story/3153904-50-years-of-saving-lives/).

DOMESTIC LIFE IN DEEP RIVER AND THE BLOND BOMBER

CHAPTER FOUR

Concurrent with the construction of the Chalk River Nuclear Laboratories (CRNL) on the Ottawa River, a new town called Deep River was built about ten kilometres west. A minimal number of trees were cleared and the town layout was carefully designed by professional planners.

Deep River was built by AECL to house CRNL employees. When I arrived there in 1957, it was a well-established community with two beaches and many other amenities. It's a scenic town with majestic pine trees lining the streets.

Being a company-owned town for many years, residents were predominately professional and technical staff from CRNL. Housing ranged from the 162-room Staff House to large two-storey detached homes near the river. The Staff House was intended for single people like myself who lived there for a short time. As a professional, I was able to move into a semi-detached two-storey house and later into a two-storey detached house as a single person. The employees paid a modest rent for the accommodation.

Deep River was roughly halfway between the larger centres of North Bay and Ottawa on Highway 17. Most of the residents had come from large cities in Canada, the United Kingdom, and other countries, so it was quite an adjustment for them to live in a small town more than a hundred kilometres from the nearest city.

They soon took advantage of the many opportunities for outdoor recreation presented by the site chosen for the town. The Ottawa River is quite wide and deep at that point, so the water flows slowly, making it more like living on a large lake than a river.

At the time the town was built, the depth of the river couldn't be determined because of narrow caverns at the bottom. Consequently, the town was named Deep River. By the time I arrived, a large number of clubs had been established to give residents opportunities to participate in sports and other forms of recreation, the arts, and a variety of hobbies, or simply to socialize. Apparently, at one time Deep River had more clubs per capita than any community in Canada.

I enjoyed my life in Deep River since its natural beauty was similar to Bruce Mines. I was active in the ski club, serving as president for a period of time during which a small ski jump was built on the local hill. It wasn't a long hill but some runs that were challenging enough to develop skills. I participated in giving free lessons to novices. Members of the club would also travel to ski on the larger hills in the Ottawa and Montreal areas.

Many of the staff at CRNL came from countries where skiing either wasn't possible or wasn't popular. Consequently, Deep River offered an opportunity to try it out. A member of the ski club once told me about a time when he was at the larger ski hill on the shore of the river. It was late fall and some snow had fallen, but the river hadn't yet frozen. The winters were cold enough that the river would eventually freeze deep enough to ski across to the Quebec side.

On this day, a man from England decided to try out his new skis, but he hadn't taken any ski lessons. I suppose he had previously seen other people skiing and thought it looked easy enough. He decided to try one of the runs that ended near the water. Not knowing how to control his speed by turning or snow-ploughing, he went straight down the hill and gathering speed as he went, skiing right into the Ottawa River. Momentarily, all that could be seen was his tam floating on the water!

Fortunately, my friend was there to help rescue him. Perhaps this was a lesson learned the hard way!

Thinking of this story made me realize that while the experience was no doubt taken as a lesson by the Englishman, I didn't consider it as a lesson for myself. The lesson I'm referring to is the fact that one should never attempt an activity for the first time that carries some risk without receiving instruction.

I remember a very embarrassing experience I had some time later, one that's associated with sailing rather than skiing. Sailing had become a very popular activity in Deep River, which also had a very active yacht club. There was a clubhouse and a long dock on the river. In the summer, a large number of sailboats would be anchored near the clubhouse. The club also held competitions and a youth training program.

Fred Moote, who worked with me in the NRU physics office, owned a small sailboat. One summer he was going away on vacation and offered to let me use his sailboat while he was away. I explained that I had never operated a sailboat, but he assured me it wasn't difficult and he would take me out to show me how to handle it. Unfortunately, there was no wind the day he took me out, so all he could demonstrate was how to put up the sail and lower it again. He explained the rest but couldn't demonstrate it. I assume he believed that was sufficient to entrust me with his boat.

The following Saturday was a beautiful sunny day with just a slight breeze, so I decided it would be a good day to go sailing.

I asked my younger brother Albert to come with me, which was the only wise thing I did in this adventure. Albert knew even less about sailing than I did.

Sailboats are steered by moving the rudder with a hinged pair of rods which permit the operator to sit on the edge of the boat while steering it. Fred had asked me to take this controller home so it wouldn't get stolen. My first mistake was to forget to take it with us; instead of going back to get it when we got to the boat, I thought it would be okay to substitute a stick I found at the beach.

I then put up the sail and found that the breeze was strong enough to slowly move the boat. I was able to steer it without a problem. Thinking this was great, I decided to sail across to the Quebec side of the river, in the direction the wind was blowing.

That was my second mistake. After anchoring at the Quebec side for a short time, I noticed the wind was starting to pick up, so I decided we should go back. Fred had explained how to manoeuvre the sail and rudder to tack into the wind, and we were doing fine for a while… but as the wind increased, we found that we couldn't keep on track to get back to the dock. When we finally got to the other side, we were quite far downriver. Realizing we couldn't sail upstream, I took the sail down and Albert and I tried using paddles, but our progress was poor.

Fortunately, another sailor in an even smaller sailboat was heading upstream and, realizing we were in trouble, came over to help. He threw out a rope and towed us back to the dock while tacking into the wind. He pulled us as close as possible to the dock, then let go of the rope and went on with his sailing.

Because of the wind we still had difficulty making progress with the paddles, so I decided to jump over the side with the rope in my hand and pull the boat in. By the time I got to the back of the sailboat and jumped in the water, we had drifted into deeper water and I dropped temporarily out of sight below the surface. Once I came up out of the water I somehow managed to pull us to the point where people on the dock could help.

I'm sure this scene produced much conversation in the clubhouse that day. Talk about embarrassment! Like the Englishman, I foolishly went for it without adequate preparation and proper consideration of the risks involved. I'm so thankful that help was there when we needed it despite my foolishness.

I was also a member of the wood-working club, through which I built a classic dogsled for my brother Edwin to use in his trapping activity north of Sudbury in the winter.

The most life-changing event during my stay in Deep River occurred when I was living in a detached house on Rutherford Avenue. Shortly after getting that house, I decided it would be best for my mother and two younger siblings to come live with me in Deep River. This would allow my sister Helen and her family to move into the old homestead in Bruce Mines.

One day I went shopping for my mother at the only grocery store in town. Now being one to browse, I moved quickly around the store with my grocery cart. At the same time, I noticed a beautiful blond teenager similarly moving quickly around the store. She was coming down another aisle that was perpendicular to the track I was on, and at the intersection of the aisles our carts crashed into each other. I apologized profusely and we went our separate ways.

To my pleasant surprise, she ended up at the same checkout line with her mother ahead of me. Her mother turned, looked at me, and spoke to me in Finnish. I remembered enough of the language to respond that although I was Finnish, I knew very little of the language. She invited me in English to come to their place for a sauna! I accepted the invitation, mainly because it would give me an opportunity to learn more about her daughter, the girl I had crashed into.

In pondering this experience, I considered it to be very unusual for someone to invite a perfect stranger over for a sauna. In any case, I did go over the next Saturday. Their home was on the outskirts of Deep River, and the sauna was a separate building on their country property. Her father had built it at the same time that he built their house. It had a wood-burning stove which was equipped with a chimney, so it wasn't a smoke sauna like the one I'd grown up with. I appreciated the opportunity to enjoy the sauna since I hadn't been able to do so in more than six years.

I learned that the girl I had crashed into was named Helen Aspila. Her mother and father were Hilda and Paavo Aspila, and both were of Finnish descent. Helen had a twin brother, Keijo, and an older brother, Kalevi.

I also discovered that I wasn't a stranger to Helen's mother or father, as I had assumed. Finnish people tend to be nationalistic and take special notice of the names of people who are likely of Finnish background. Helen's father, Paavo Aspila, worked at the plant as a carpenter. Somehow he was aware of my name, and he may have seen me at the plant. Her mother had been keeping an eye out for me when she was in town.

That first Saturday visit led to many other invitations to have a sauna and watch hockey games. Helen's mother was a keen hockey fan, becoming even more so later as more and more Finns came to play in the NHL. Helen was still in high school at this time, so she would often be doing homework rather than joining in to watch hockey. But Kalevi befriended me and we participated in many outdoor activities together with another Finnish friend, Henry Hollo. Henry's parents owned a cottage on the river and had a separate non-smoke sauna. The three of us would enjoy a sauna at times and then go for a dip in the river, even when it was too cold for swimming.[7]

I learned that Helen had become involved in playing golf at the age of twelve. Kalevi had helped her make her first golf club, putting together several pieces of lumber that resembled a club. In the sandy foundation where their new home was to be built, she banged out golf balls, and sometimes tennis balls. They were easy to retrieve as the balls would become embedded in the sandy banks.

Mr. McPherson, the local pro, offered free golf lessons for juniors in Deep River and Helen took advantage of them. By then she had a set of golf clubs and had developed her skills to the point where she often won tournaments.

I was smitten by Helen when I first laid eyes on her and the attraction grew every time I interacted with her. To enhance our opportunities to interact, I bought a set of golf clubs and began playing golf, hoping Helen might be willing to give me some lessons. She did. Gradually, she joined me in outings like going to movies with me and her brothers. Since we were all blond, some townsfolks thought I was a relative, which was prophetic since she ended up marrying me when she was nineteen after three years of dating; we did actually become family.

During conversations with the Aspila family, I learned that Helen's folks felt some resentment over the fact that living in Deep River itself wasn't an option for them. The company would only allow employees who were professionals and tradespeople holding supervisory roles to rent company homes in town. Some townspeople had referred to people like the Aspilas as "highway bums." Helen's mother could have felt some hesitation about inviting me over for a sauna knowing that I was a single professional who had been given a detached home to rent in town.

---

[7]   This is a common practice in Finland.

Considering the improbability of the sequence of events leading up to this marriage, it's clearly another example of God's grace in operation. It was the union of a dynamic and competitive extrovert and an introverted scientist. We complemented each other.

I married Helen in the Deep River Community Church. Helen had been confirmed in the Lutheran Church through a correspondence course given by a Finnish Lutheran pastor in Kirkland Lake. However, her family weren't attending the Lutheran Church in Deep River and her mother requested that the wedding be conducted by a Kirkland Lake Finnish pastor they knew. I had no problem with that. The service was conducted in Finnish, so Helen and I didn't understand much of what was being said, but we knew enough to say our "I do's" at the right time. A reception was held in the Aspilas' basement which her dad had put a lot of work into preparing for the occasion.

Helen and I were married five years after I came to Deep River, almost to the day, and immediately following the wedding and honeymoon we went to live in an apartment in suburban Toronto with my mother and younger brother Albert, who was still attending high school. I had decided to apply for a job opening posted at CRNL for a reactor physicist in the Nuclear Power Plant Division of Atomic Energy of Canada, and I was accepted. This was a team of engineers and scientists in Etobicoke assembled to design commercial nuclear power stations for Ontario Hydro, whose head office was in downtown Toronto. Being aware of their plans to build a series of nuclear power stations, I believed that joining this team would provide more opportunities for advancement than at CRNL, since there were no plans to build more research reactors after NRU. Helen knew that I had applied and was fine with that. I was determined to make this change in my career when Helen agreed to marry me.

In retrospect I realized how selfish I was not to consider the degree of adjustment she would have to face. Helen had grown up in a small town in northern Ontario called Larder Lake, living there until she was nine. It was a beautiful natural environment like Deep River, and they'd lived close to the lake. They'd enjoyed fishing off a dock and swimming in the summer.

Like my father, her dad had to work away from home a lot. He worked in a gold mine for a time in Kirkland Lake, until his friend Mr. Maki died in a mining accident. After that, he sought work elsewhere, including a long period on the construction of a large, well-known log hotel at Montebello, Quebec. He heard about the CRNL project and decided to move to Deep River and get steady work as a carpenter at the plant.

Helen had received a lot of recognition for her achievements as a competitive golfer, but suddenly she found herself in a brick and mortar apartment building in a big city living with a mother-in-law and a brother-in-law! The scene from the living room window included homes with a sea of TV antennas on roofs. Talk about culture shock.

It turned out she was up to the challenge, demonstrating the Finnish concept of *sisu*, which is discussed at length in Katja Pantzar's *The Finnish Way*.[8] It's a combination of determination (*päättäväisyys*) patience (*kärsivällisyys*), stamina (*kestävyys*), and power (*voima*).

Helen was much like her mother in many ways. At one of her Mackenzie High School reunions, her former principal, Mr. Caruthers, shared with her that he had been very impressed with her mother, who had been his domestic helper. She had even

---

[8] Pantzar, *The Finnish Way* (New York, NY: Tarcher Perigee Penguin Random House, 2018). When you read the history of Finland, you soon learn how resilient and courageous the Finns have had to be.

motivated him to go on a vacation to Finland to experience the Finnish culture and meet many more Finns.

Her fascination for the world around her led Helen to take many courses and attend numerous conferences throughout her life. Shortly after arriving in Toronto, she enrolled at Burnhamthorpe Collegiate to take an accounting course which proved beneficial in future retail opportunities and handling our finances. To improve her speaking skills, she took a public speaking course. She also received an award for being the number one speaker at the end of the term. She took multiple courses to become a certified Christian counsellor. To keep our rototiller operating for more than thirty years, she took a small engines course and overhauled the tiller, installing an electric starter.

Seeing the depletion of forests worldwide, she even tried saving every tree seedling on our country property in Erin, Ontario, where we lived for thirty-four years. She saw the environmental connection and importance of trees long before the worldwide pollution crisis developed, which started killing thousands of people and animals.

She is a natural environmentalist, always combating deforestation. Even after we moved to Brantford, seedlings kept popping up in our gardens and lawn. It seemed they knew they would be taken care of or be transplanted into a safe haven where they could grow to maturity, taking in carbon dioxide and releasing oxygen.

Her adaptation to changes in life, as well as changes in my career, was phenomenal.

As she began studying Christianity in all aspects, she became intrigued with the Person of Jesus Christ, God's Son. When God started showing up and revealing Himself to her, she took more courses and became an ordained minister at the age of fifty.

Her spiritual knowledge and understanding had a profound effect on me as well. While I was pursuing the physics and physical laws of the earth, she connected with the spiritual laws and the Person behind them! She saw the connection between the two long before I did. Reading God's Holy Word was a thrill to her, as she saw much wisdom in its pages.

Somewhere along her quest to know God, she was sent a quote made by Albert Einstein back in the late 1920s as he was interviewed by a journalist from the *Saturday Evening Post*. This is what he said about the New Testament: "No one can read the Gospels without feeling the actual presence of Jesus. His personality pulsates in every word. No myth is filled with such life."[9] Helen was awestruck, as this came from one of the greatest Jewish scientists in the world and a person whose mathematical formulae I used in my nuclear physics studies.

Finnish *sisu*, as practiced by Helen, factored into many fascinating adventures and challenges in our long marriage. She realizes that *sisu* as being connected to the one true God who is her strength and joy.

I had no idea how my life would transpire living with my "blond bomber." Later in our marriage, I came to think of her as my virtuous Proverbs 31 wife!

On one of our vacations later in our marriage, she informed me that we would be purchasing a piece of land. Would you believe it? The timing of the purchase was perfect, because two years later we made a substantial profit from the sale of that small piece of land. The profit covered the cost of yard equipment, including a new tractor.

---

[9]   Albert Einstein, "No one can read the Gospels..." *Goodreads*. Date of access: April 26, 2021 (https://www.goodreads.com/quotes/10670843-no-one-can-read-the-gospels-without-feeling-the-actual).

WORK IN
THE BIG CITY

CHAPTER FIVE

As a result of my decision to change jobs and move to the big city, we found ourselves facing a huge transition. Every weekday, I had to fight traffic to get to work. AECL had rented a large Quonset-type building from Ontario Hydro to house the power reactor design team. It had few windows and was located in an industrial area of Etobicoke. This was quite a change from the beautiful view of the Ottawa River I had enjoyed at CRNL.

However, as I learned of the scope of the project I would be working on, my physical surroundings became a secondary concern. New facilities were under construction at Sheridan Park Research Centre in Mississauga which included a large office building and a laboratory where testing would be done in support of the engineering design work. The move took place within two years of me joining the team and it brought about a huge improvement in our work environment.

When I joined the design team in Etobicoke, the design of the second nuclear power station for Ontario Hydro had been completed and construction was nearing completion. It was located on the east shore of Lake Huron. The locals identified the location as Douglas Point, so that was the name given to the power station.

Ontario was in a hurry to start drawing on nuclear electric power. Consequently, planning for the Douglas Point reactor started early in 1957, when I was still at university. It was the first of the next generation of nuclear electric stations. The design capacity was ten times that of NPD. The ones to follow would have an even higher output.

The initial design for the prototype NPD reactor had placed the natural uranium fuel rods in a large pressurized steel vessel with thick walls to withstand the high pressure required. The timing of the Douglas Point design process was fortunate because it was determined that a scale-up of the NPD design would require a pressure vessel that was too big, too expensive, and possibly unsafe.

This was a crisis. Research showed that the NPD reactor, which had been intended to be a full prototype for future reactors, risked being a technological dead end. Thus a difficult but very necessary decision was made to terminate all work on the NPD design. This turned out to be a gamechanger, because it led to the very clever idea of substituting individual pressure tubes, each containing a string of fuel bundles for the pressure vessel. With this approach, scaling up to larger reactors simply meant increasing the number of pressure tubes. If this decision hadn't been made, the very successful CANDU power reactor program I contributed to wouldn't have happened.

I worked in the reactor physics section of the Physics and Analysis Department of the Nuclear Power Plant Division of AECL. Staff in this section had the responsibility to develop computer software that would simulate the nuclear processes occurring in the core of the reactor where the energy was produced by atom splitting, converting some mass to energy. This was critical in the design process because it was the only way to know if a specific design of the core would yield a self-sustaining chain reaction on a continuing basis. This section was also responsible for calculating the thickness of the radiation shielding material around the core and other systems necessary to reduce radiation levels to acceptable values. In addition, software had to be developed for use by reactor operators to schedule uranium fuel replacement.

The team in Etobicoke was established in 1959 to design the Douglas Point Nuclear Power Reactor, the first commercial-scale reactor in Canada. This bold project put Canada into the world nuclear power scene along with the United Kingdom, which was building two 300-megawatt Magnox reactors, and the United States, which had the 60-megawatt Shippingport PWR reactor and was building a 200-megawatt BWR.

Dr. John Foster, the project manager for the Douglas Point project, had managed the NPD project for Canadian General Electric in Peterborough, Ontario. He later became President of AECL.

When I joined the team in the fall of 1962, the reactor physics analysis required to design the core had been completed, but the engineering design process had resulted in minor differences in characteristics of the core from what had been used in earlier physics analysis. I was assigned the task of determining what the impact of these differences would be on the refuelling rate required to keep the reactor operating at full power.

The refuelling rate is a very important factor in the economics of using nuclear energy to produce electricity. The fuel cost per kilowatt hour of electricity is proportional to the refuelling rate. I'm sure that in the first nuclear power proposal made by W.B. Lewis at CRNL in the early 1950s a strong case was made that the quantity of natural uranium needed per megawatt day (MWD) of electrical energy produced would be extremely low, due to the fact that the energy came from the conversion of mass to energy according to $E=MC^2$. The speed of light (C) is a big number—299,792,458 meters per second. Modelling of the physics characteristics of an operating reactor at a point in time includes determination of the energy produced in each fuel bundle by the time it is discharged from the fuel channel. It is converted to MWD of electrical energy produced per tonne of uranium in the discharged fuel. The average value for all fuel discharged is called the average discharge burnup.

After completing the analysis, resulting in an estimate of the average discharge burnup for the as-built reactor, I reported the result to my boss, Liberty Pease, in a memorandum. Knowing Dr. Lewis would want to know about it, he sent him a copy of my memorandum.

In a few days, I was very surprised to receive a direct phone call from Dr. Lewis. I had heard a lot about him while at CRNL but had no direct interaction with him. Several times he had been on the same company bus as me, and he always carried a briefcase bulging with documents.

Dr. Lewis had never married and was very devoted to his work. He was known as the father of nuclear energy in Canada. He apparently was known to speak directly with the people who performed the analysis, rather than that person's superiors.

Well, he obviously hadn't heard about me when I worked in NRU, because the first words he said to me on the phone were "Who are you?" Before I had a chance to answer, he started talking about the Douglas Point discharge burnup, implying that I wasn't qualified to be involved in calculating it. He finished by sternly declaring, "It shall be 10,000 MWD/TeU!"[10] The value I had reported was 8,400 MWD/TeU.

I later learned that Dr. Lewis had widely publicized that Douglas Point was designed to yield 10,000 MWD/TeU.

---

[10]   MWD/TeU refers to megawatt days per tonne of uranium.

I was quite relieved to learn much later that the actual average burnup was close to 8,400, the figure I had predicted. Of course, I never heard from Dr. Lewis again! I don't know if he had any further conversations with my boss about it.

Douglas Point began generating electricity in 1967 and continued until 1984. The success of this project put Canada into the export field of commercial nuclear power when a duplicate station at Rajasthan, India was committed in 1963. The confidence of Ontario Hydro in the design capabilities of the Nuclear Power Plant Division led to them being granted a major role in the design of the first two 520-megawatt Pickering reactors, also in 1963. The site near Pickering on Lake Ontario eventually saw eight 520-megawatt reactors. They were constructed from 1965 to 1986.

The early success of the Pickering reactors demonstrated that the CANDU nuclear plants produced electricity economically and with no CO_2 emissions, since carbon combustion was replaced by nuclear fission. This led Ontario Hydro to construct another eight-unit station on the east shore of Lake Huron south of Douglas Point. It was named the Bruce Nuclear Plant after the county it was located in.

The nameplate capacity of these reactors varies from 830 megawatts to 891 megawatts, almost double that of Pickering. They were constructed from 1969 to 1987.

However, even this was insufficient to eliminate coal-fired generation in Ontario and meet the projected demand for electricity as the Ontario economy grew. The last nuclear power station to be built in Ontario as of 2020 was a four-unit station built on the north shore of Lake Ontario East of Pickering. These reactors had a capacity similar to the Bruce reactors. It was constructed from 1981 to 1993 and was called the Darlington Station. All these reactors were natural uranium CANDU reactors patterned after Pickering.

The Nuclear Power Plant Division of AECL had a predominant role in the design of Pickering. Ontario Hydro had been building their own design team in addition to operations staff to work at the stations. The design team included physicists and other specialists who could do analysis work similar to what was done in the Safety and Analysis Department I was part of. Most of the Bruce reactor's core design work was done by my group in conjunction with the Ontario Hydro counterparts. In the case of Darlington, most was done by Ontario Hydro.

In parallel with doing the work for the Ontario Hydro reactors, AECL launched a campaign to design and market a 600-megawatt capacity CANDU reactor. Because of the success of the Ontario Hydro program, utilities in Quebec and New Brunswick had one constructed at Trois Rivière, Quebec, which operated from 1983 until 2012, and another at Point LePreau, New Brunswick, which has been in operation since 1983.

Marketing initiatives resulted in several copies being constructed in South Korea, China, Romania, and Argentina. It should be evident that this intensity of CANDU design, construction, commissioning, and to a lesser extent operation activity demanded a rapid increase of staff in the Nuclear Power Plant Division. This was true in the Safety and Analysis Department as well, which created opportunities for people to advance into managerial roles.

I was given a variety of management roles over my twenty-nine years in the CANDU program.[11]

---

[11] See Appendix.

CAN DO CANDU

CHAPTER SIX

The Canadian nuclear power reactors were identified as CANDU reactors because their design was unique in the world. The name is a short form of Canadian Deuterium Uranium, and they are the only power reactor design that employs deuterium oxide, or heavy water, as a moderator and coolant.

The development of this technology goes back to the decision taken in the 1940s for Canada to establish the science needed to design the core of power reactors that could use natural uranium for fuel. Experiments had shown natural uranium would only work if a moderator of heavy water or graphite was used. It was decided that England would focus on graphite (Magnox reactors) and Canada on heavy water (CANDU reactors).

What is a moderator? As mentioned in the introduction, neutrons released in fission are high-energy. The physics of the process is such that it would be necessary to have a very high concentration of fissile atoms present to produce a self-sustaining chain reaction in the material by itself. An example is the atomic bomb, in which the energy source is almost a hundred percent fissile material, such as U335 or fissile plutonium. The reactions are produced by very high-energy neutrons, which results in an extremely fast, exponential increase in energy produced when a critical mass is achieved.

With natural uranium, the concentration of U235 atoms is much too low for this to happen. If the kinetic energy of the neutrons could be greatly lowered, the probability of causing fission is much higher.

Therefore, a medium is provided in the reactor, called the moderator, which slows down the neurons. The best moderating materials are those containing a high density of nuclei having nearly the same mass as the neutrons themselves. The reason for this is that the slowing down process is the result of elastic collision of the neutrons with the nuclei of the moderator, and the maximum transfer of kinetic energy from a high-velocity particle to a lower speed or stationary particle takes place if the masses of the particles are the same.[12]

Of course, this criterion alone would make H2O the best moderator since the hydrogen atoms have nearly the same mass as neutrons. However, it turns out that ordinary water simply doesn't work as a moderator in a natural uranium reactor because the proportion of neutrons captured by the hydrogen nuclei, and thus lost to the chain reaction, is too high compared to those that are merely slowed down. The deuterium nuclei, on the other hand, are quite effective in slowing down neutrons, but the probability of it capturing a neutron is a thousand times less than that for hydrogen. These two effects are combined in a parameter called the moderating power. The value for ordinary water is 62, heavy water is 5,000, and graphite is 165. This means that heavy water is the best moderator in the world.

The Pickering CANDU reactor core is a large cylindrical tank called a calandria. The ends have an array of holes drilled in an equally spaced pattern. Tubes called calandria tubes, having

---

[12]   Billiards present a good example of this principle.

the same diameter as the holes, are welded at each end. The calandria then can be filled with heavy water. Pressure tubes are inserted in the calandria tubes, into which are loaded a string of twelve fuel bundles. A Pickering fuel bundle is a cluster of twenty-eight fuel elements, each containing natural uranium dioxide pellets inside a zircaloy tube called a sheath with closed ends. The figure on page 50 shows the Pickering 28 element bundle design as well as the designs for NPD, Douglas Point, and the higher capacity CANDU reactors, which is also the one shown in the enlargement. The one labeled "CANFLEX" is a design considered for future advanced fuel cycle CANDU reactors. The heavy water in the calandria is the moderator. To minimize the number of neutrons that simply leak out of the calandria, it is made large enough to provide a blanket of heavy water between the outermost calandria tubes and the tank wall. This annular region is called the reflector. An early task of reactor physicists in the design process is to determine the number and spacing of the fuel channels and the reflector thickness to achieve the necessary power rating of the plant with the best neutron economy. This sets the diameter of the calandria needed.

Heavy water is very costly to produce, so systems containing heavy water are designed to prevent leaks. The calandria isn't a pressure vessel because the moderator is operated at a low temperature so it can easily be designed to be leak-tight.

Feeder piping is connected to the pressure tubes at each end of the calandria and pass through a steam generator to provide a closed circulating system of pressurized heavy water coolant. This system carries heat energy produced in the fuel into a steam generator where the heat energy is transferred to lower pressure H_2O, converting it to steam which is used to drive turbines to produce electricity. The steam then goes through a condenser to cool it back to liquid water which in turn is pumped back into the steam generator. Lake water is circulated through the condenser to condense the steam and then it is returned to the lake. The heavy water coolant must be operated at a high enough pressure to prevent it from boiling, and the coolant piping system must be of high integrity to prevent leaks, because of the cost of heavy water.

The fuel bundles are moved through the pressure tubes with a robot called the fuelling machine, located at each end of the calandria. The fuel is moved in opposite directions in adjacent channels. This is necessary to keep the ratio of the maximum bundle power to the core average at a minimum value. It is the maximum bundle power in the core that determines the power capacity of the reactor because the temperature of the fuel cannot be allowed to exceed a safe value.

There is a great deal more to the engineering design of a nuclear plant than the reactor core. The figure on page 51 is a schematic of a CANDU Power Plant.[13]

One of the goals of the reactor physics analysis is to define design specifications for all the systems in the core needed to operate the reactor safely while maintaining a minimum peak to average bundle power ratio, and maximum average discharge burnup of the fuel.

As section head of reactor physics, and later as branch manager, I had the responsibility of supervising a group of physicists, many with PhDs, to develop the computer software needed to model the reactor core with sufficient accuracy to evaluate various options for the design of control and safety systems, in-core instrumentation, and fuel management strategies.

---

[13]   A detailed description of the design of a CANDU reactor is presented in: Roger Steed, BSc P.Eng., *Nuclear Power in Canada and Beyond* (Renfrew, ON: General Store Publishing House, 2007).

The evolution of digital computing capability was at a very early stage at the time Pickering was being designed. In fact, while at university we had to do digital programming using Boolean algebra. At CRNL, most of my analytical work was done using a slide rule, which I still have. A mechanical calculator was used for most of my early analytical work on CANDU reactors. The degree of detail to which the reactor could be digitally modelled was greatly limited because of computer memory and speed.

It was particularly important to be able to predict the power distribution in the core, because that would determine the size of the calandria needed to house the amount of fuel required to achieve the desired power rating of the reactor. To calculate the power distribution in a nuclear reactor, it is necessary to determine the spatial variation of the neutron density, which is proportional to the power. The neutron density is affected by the composition of atoms throughout the core as well as the probability of the atoms capturing a neutron. The problem is compounded by the fact that there are hundreds of different atoms produced from the fission of U235, Pu239, and Pu241.[14] Concentrations of these atoms vary with time in each fuel bundle. Neutron absorption in the in-core hardware must also be accounted for.

Because physicists were aware of the extreme complexity of the nuclear reactions occurring in an operating reactor at the beginning of the nuclear era, it was realized that it would be necessary to do a lot of experimental work in research reactors first. The work done at CRNL, as well as in other nuclear laboratories, generated the data that permitted physicists like Eugene Critoph at CRNL to develop semiempirical formulations which were validated experimentally.

---

[14]   The plutonium fissile isotopes are produced from neutron capture in U238. In fact, about half of the energy produced in CANDU reactors comes from splitting plutonium isotopes.

The computer software resulting from this work was applied in the NPD and Douglas Point core designs. My staff and I made modifications to the software to make it more efficient and intuitive to apply in the Pickering analysis. This permitted us to calculate the reaction rates in a unit cell, which included the fuel bundle, pressure tube, calandria tube, and some moderator, for potentially each bundle in the core at any point in its movement through the core. This software was used in reactor physics analysis for the rest of my tenure with AECL.

It is interesting that my master's thesis, "Calculating the Resonance Escape Probability in Nuclear Reactions Using the Monte Carlo Theory," proposed a way to calculate one of the key parameters in a unit cell calculation in a very accurate way when computing capability would permit it.

The parameter is called the Resonance Escape Probability. Natural uranium has two isotopes of uranium, 238 and 235. These numbers represent the total number of neutrons and protons in the atom of natural uranium. More than ninety-eight percent is U238. The small amount of U235 is the reason a CANDU reactor works. If a U235 atom absorbs a low-energy neutron, it has a high probability of splitting (fissioning). This results in some of the mass being converted to energy according to Einstein's equation $E=MC^2$. Fission results in two or three free neutrons being released in the process of dividing into two smaller atoms. If more than one of these neutrons is absorbed in a U235 atom, a multiplying chain reaction occurs. Unfortunately, the much higher concentration of U238, as well as the fission products and structural and other material in the reactor, can absorb neutrons without causing a fission, resulting in less than one neutron being absorbed in U235.

The task of the nuclear reactor physicist is to find a way to calculate all the reaction rates happening in a specific reactor design to determine if a chain reaction is possible and how long it can be sustained until the uranium fuel has to be replaced.

The reaction rate of neutrons with U238 is dependent on the neutron energy. Neutrons released in U235 fission are very high-energy and have to be slowed down by colliding with other atoms to increase the probability of being absorbed in U235 atoms. Water is effective in slowing down neutrons. Heavy water—or D2O, since deuterium is twice as heavy as hydrogen—is needed in order to use natural uranium in a CANDU-type reactor. Water (H2O) is used in many reactors in the world, but they have to use fuel artificially enriched in U235 since H2O absorbs more neutrons than D2O. U238 has the characteristic that the probability of capturing a neutron as a function of its energy has a big spike at a specific energy, which is called resonance energy. This is similar to what happens when sound interacts with physical objects. Calculating the probability of neutron capture rate at this energy level is critical to determine whether a chain reaction will occur.

The most direct way to determine this probability would be to somehow track the interaction sequence of each individual neutron from the point of release in fission through the point when it collides with water and other atoms, all the while slowing down, to determine how many will strike a U238 atom at the resonance energy.

I had found in the scientific literature that visionaries were postulating that digital computing speeds and memory could someday reach the point where this type of methodology could be practically applied to very complex chains of events. Because it depends heavily on determining probabilities, they coined this the "Monte Carlo method." My thesis outlined how it might be applied specifically to determining the resonance escape probability.

A few years after I retired from AECL, I heard from my former staff that it was beginning to be applied by the reactor physics group in reactor design analysis.

I was elated to see the idea from my thesis come to fruition in my lifetime. I give much credit to people like Eugene Critoph at Chalk River who developed the semiempirical formulas for calculating the reaction rates, including the resonance escape probability which I and my staff used to produce the software we used in the design of the CANDU cores. The computer simulations of the reaction rates in the reactors turned out to be surprisingly accurate in actual reactor operation. This was no doubt due to the fact that the formulations were based on a great deal of experimental data and could be tested in the research reactors at CRNL.

Software needed to be developed to calculate the neutron density (power) distribution in the complete core using the reaction rates from the unit cell program. This software was developed by staff in the Reactor Physics Branch more skilled in nuclear physics and mathematics than I was. Because of computer speed and memory limitations, the power distribution could only be crudely modelled.

Nuclear power reactors require in-core hardware and instrumentation to operate safely. This includes devices for regulating the power during normal power operation and safety devices to rapidly shut down the reactor when it is unsafe to keep operating. These devices are oriented vertically and require hollow tubes to be inserted between fuel channels to isolate them from the moderator. Regulating devices are in the core during normal operation and the safety devices are outside the core.

A major responsibility of the reactor physics team was to determine the location and composition of the regulating and safety devices necessary for them to accomplish their nuclear performance specifications. This required a lot of interaction with the design engineers responsible for their physical design.

Any non-fissile material in the core negatively impacts the power distribution and the average discharge burnup of the fuel because it removes neutrons out of the fission chain reactions; consequently, fixed hardware in the core should be made of material having a low probability of capturing neutrons. However, it also has to have the required structural integrity. This resulted in new alloys being researched and tested that are unique to the CANDU reactors.

An example is an alloy called zircaloy, which is an alloy of zirconium which has a lower probability of capturing neutrons than other structural materials like steel.

It wasn't possible to develop computer models to accurately simulate the effect of individual regulating systems devices on the power distribution in the core because of digital computer limitations at the time Pickering was designed. Therefore, the task of specifying the location and length of the control rods was challenging. I had my staff run a number of crude two- and three-dimensional simulations using the software they had developed. It was my responsibility to use the resulting data to recommend the core layout of the control and safety devices.

In the next chapter, I will explain how it was possible to measure the neutron population distribution along a central fuel channel following the first start-up of the first Pickering reactor. When I learned that this unique method agreed closely with the design's objective, I was very happy. Other physics measurements also agreed well, which I attribute to answered prayer, because of the degree of judgment needed in making recommendations for the design.

I was particularly thankful that it turned out this way because, after preparing the memorandum specifying the core layout of control and safety systems, I expected it would receive in-depth review by my boss and peers. Instead my boss called me into his office after reading it, thanked me, and stated, "Art, this is your Rubicon"—meaning the design would proceed based on my recommendation. There would be no turning back.

Another major responsibility of the Reactor Physics Branch was related to fuel management. We had to develop software that could be used by Ontario Hydro to establish a schedule for replacing the fuel one or more bundles at a time. Online bidirectional fuelling provided an opportunity to use the fuel management strategy to reduce the peak to average bundle power and hence allow a higher reactor power rating for a given size of core. This was accomplished by moving the fuel through the central channels more slowly than outer ones. This resulted in a central region of the core having a higher discharge burnup than the outer. Refuelling adjacent channels in opposite directions meant that it was easy to maintain axial symmetry in the power distribution.

I believe the successful outcome of the Pickering core design was a significant factor in it setting the pattern for the CANDU designs that followed. The Bruce and CANDU 600 designs had different size cores and other variations, so a lot of physics analysis was required for them as well. Computing speed and memory increased rapidly, making more detailed modelling of the whole core possible. My staff produced several computer programs based on diffusion theory.

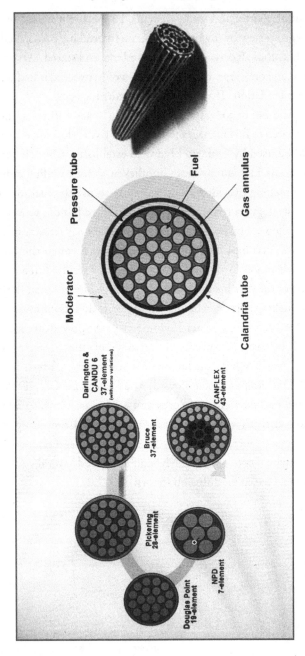

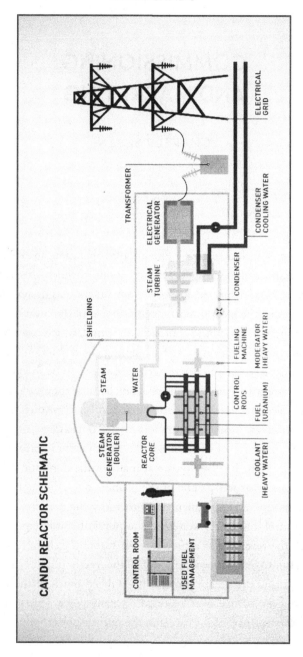

COMMISSIONING
AND MARKETING

CHAPTER SEVEN

B efore a nuclear reactor is first put into operation, an extensive commissioning program is carried out in which all systems are tested and inspected to ensure they function as designed. In my opinion, the most important component of the commissioning program is the initial approach-to-critical, which culminates in the reactor achieving a self-sustaining chain reaction for the first time. Reactor physicists necessarily need to be involved in this part of the commissioning program because they understand the physics characteristics of the reactor and can give direction to the station operators to ensure it is carried out safely.

As manager of the Reactor Physics Branch, I had the opportunity to be involved onsite at many of the domestic CANDU reactors, as well as two of the offshore ones, during the initial start-up and subsequent tests to verify the performance of the control and safety systems. The physical conditions under which the reactor first achieved a self-sustaining chain reaction was a litmus test of the accuracy of all the reactor physics analysis done during the design process. It validated much of the work done by my branch over a period of many years. This was the most exciting part of my career in the nuclear power industry.

Pickering was particularly exciting and rewarding because it was the first project I worked on from start to finish, including the physics-related commissioning. I was responsible for preparing the physics test procedures in conjunction with reactor physics staff at Ontario Hydro.

Because I was fully aware of the limitations of the computer modelling of the control rods, I considered it very important to find a way to measure the neutron population distribution in detail in the core during low-power commissioning. The nuclear research program had resulted in instrumentation that could measure neutron population and radiation at very low levels. The Pickering fuel bundle had twenty-eight elements arranged in a way that left a space in the centre (see the figure on page 50).

During my work at CRNL, I had some interaction with Dr. Al Okazaki, an experimental physicist who had worked on experiments in the ZEEP and Zed-2 low-power research reactors.[15] I knew he had used activation of a copper wire to measure neutron density in research reactors. When copper absorbs neutrons, a radioactive isotope is produced. Measurement of the radiation emitted by the wire indicates the variation of neutron density in the region of the reactor where the wire has been inserted.

Since there is enough space to insert a copper wire into the centre of the fuel bundle, I asked Al to look for a way to insert a wire the full length of the central fuel channel. He found a very simple but clever way to do it, which was approved by Ontario Hydro. This provided invaluable and very detailed information to improve the accuracy of computer modelling of nuclear reactors.

---

[15] These were both natural uranium fuelled and heavy water moderated experimental reactors. ZEEP went critical in 1945 and was the second reactor in the world to do so. Zed-2 went critical in 1960. ZEEP was instrumental in the development of the NRX and NRU research reactors, and Zed-2 for the CANDU power reactors.

The Pickering fuel design was the only one where this was permitted to be done. Of course, the fact that it validated my choice of the control rod locations made me very thankful that it was approved by Ontario Hydro. I had a great working relationship with Dr. John Brenciaglia, who was my counterpart at Ontario Hydro.

Two other of my experiences with the low-power commissioning were particularly memorable.

First, I was involved with the reactor physics analysis for a reactor in Rajasthan, India, which was a copy of the Douglas Point reactor in Ontario, the first one that was designed by AECL and Ontario Hydro.

When it came time to start up the Indian reactor, I was assigned the task of planning and managing the implementation of the initial commissioning program, in which detailed tests were conducted to verify the physics analysis that formed the basis of the design. I was the only Canadian physicist at the site for that and was assisted by Indian physicists, some of whom had received training in my branch.

After all the functional tests on the hardware and software of the plant were complete, the next step was to slowly raise the level of the heavy water moderator in the calandria containing the uranium fuel (the core) while monitoring the population of neutrons in the core with very sensitive instrumentation. This is a measure of the rate of splitting of uranium atoms, and hence the energy being produced.

The prior analysis done with computer software had produced a prediction of the core volume that would result in what was called criticality, the condition where a sustained chain reaction takes place, creating a constant power level. A small increase in the core volume above that would produce a power runaway, unless compensated by operation of the reactor-regulating system. The Indian station operators, many of whom had received training in Canada, were responsible for the hands-on operation of the reactor system.

My role was to observe and supervise, with the authority to command when needed. Because the process of raising the heavy water level in the calandria was necessarily very slow, I wasn't always in the control room. Once when I walked into the control room I found all the operators heading out! I asked angrily where they were going and they answered, "It's teatime." At such a critical time, they were thinking of tea instead of safety!

I was present at the right moment to avert an outcome that could possibly have been serious, because the water level in the tank was still increasing, albeit very slowly, while they were leaving the control room. This was God's grace at work. When I explained the potential safety implications of what they were doing, they quickly rectified the situation. That experience, coupled with the fact that the Indian reactor physicists had demonstrated that they wouldn't question my judgment, made me realize the magnitude of the responsibility I carried. I had no backup on technical decisions related to the physics of the reactor. I had to stand on the promise of God that He would *"meet all [my] needs according to the riches of his glory in Christ Jesus"* (Philippians 4:19)

When I first arrived at the reactor site, I got to work on preparations for the start-up. The Indians had requested that the control rods, which are in the core during normal operation, be made of cobalt instead of steel, as they were in Douglas Point, so radioactive cobalt-60 could be produced for them. The Indian physicists had done a lot of work over a period of a year to determine the effect of this design change on the performance of the control rods in the reactor. Knowing the actual performance characteristics of the steel rods in Douglas Point, I made my own assessment of the cobalt rods on my handheld scientific calculator.

My assessment didn't agree with the Indian assessment, and the actual performance measured as part of the commissioning program turned out to be very close to my prediction.

On a trip back to our quarters with one of the Indian physicists, he turned to me and asked, "Are you some kind of god? How do you know so much?"

I seized the opportunity to tell him about the one true God who guided me. When one is in relationship with our heavenly Father, *"His God instructs him and teaches him the right way"* (Isaiah 28:26). I give God the glory for the knowledge He imparts. As Isaiah 28:29 tells us, *"All this also comes from the Lord Almighty, whose plan is wonderful, whose wisdom is magnificent."*

The second memorable experience I had during an initial start-up serves as a vivid example of the importance of checking out the nuclear physics characteristics of reactors at the extremely low-power levels that instrumentation permits.

I was responsible for the supervision of the physics tests during the start-up of the prototype reactor called BLW-250 in Trois Rivières, Quebec in the early 1970s. This was a very different design from the other CANDU reactors in Canada in that the fuel channels were vertical instead of horizontal and the coolant was natural water rather than heavy water. Also, the coolant was allowed to boil in the core, hence the name; BLW stands for "boiling light water."

The initial approach-to-critical was done without any water in the fuel channels as part of the process to verify the physics models used in the design. Cooling the fuel wasn't a concern, because it could be done at a power level of a few watts.

As in the India case, the heavy water moderator was slowly raised in the calandria, which contained the fuel channels, while we monitored the change in neutron population. The physics is such that a graph of the inverse of the population of neutrons versus the moderator level is a straight line; the level at which criticality would occur can therefore be known well before that level is reached.

During this process, I became very concerned because the graph showed that the critical level was going to be significantly higher than had been predicted from the computer modelling done by my staff. Rather than assuming this was because of the modelling limitations and allowing the process to continue until criticality was reached, I believe I was prompted by the Holy Spirit to suggest to the start-up manager that the process be terminated until I could examine other possible causes besides modelling inaccuracy.

After determining the magnitude of discrepancy on the core neutron multiplication factor, I compared it mentally to the effect on the multiplication factor of materials that might have been put into the reactor by mistake. I remembered that the effect of all the fuel channels being filled with water was double the discrepancy. For safety reasons, the coolant system had been designed so only half the channels could be filled or drained at a time; therefore, I explained to the manager that the measured multiplication factor would be that predicted by the physics analysis if half of the fuel channels were filled with water.

The staff was immediately asked to check the coolant system to make sure all the channels had been drained. Sure enough, they found that a valve on one of the loops feeding half of the channels hadn't been opened, so they were full of water. If this hadn't been discovered and the start-up proceeded to criticality, and if an operator had then realized the valve hadn't been opened as per prior instructions, and if he had decided to open it without checking with the manager, it would have resulted in half the channels being drained which then would have made the reactor super critical. A power excursion could have happened!

Obviously, we terminated the start-up program so corrective measures could be taken.

It is important to point out that when I talk about a potential super critical power excursion, this would not result in a nuclear explosion, as with a nuclear weapon. The physics wouldn't allow it. This is because the neutron speed associated with the multiplication from fission in a well-moderated reactor like CANDU fission is so low that the rate of increase in the power resulting from super criticality would be low enough to permit practical safety systems to limit the results of an operator error. The defence in depth design of CANDU safety systems is recognized as the safest in the world and more than fifty years of operating experience supports that.

The reactor subsequently did reach criticality at close to the predicted moderator level with all the channels drained. The low-power physics tests were completed without incident, so the commissioning of the reactor proceeded to the higher power phase. At a power level high enough to produce boiling of the coolant, we saw evidence of a neutronic instability developing that hadn't been predicted by the design analysis.

On my way home to Mississauga, I sat beside the engineering mastermind whose brainchild this new prototype was. He asked me about the implication of these results on full power operation and I told him that I believed controllability would be a problem.

The reactor did eventually operate at full power with some controllability issues for a time, but operation was sporadic for various reasons, including an extended shutdown in which the control rod positions were changed to hopefully improve controllability. However, the reactor remained difficult to control. By 1977, it was clear that concern about control would preclude the commitment of any larger natural uranium-fuelled CANDU

BLWs. The decision was eventually made to permanently shut down the reactor in April 1979. This design had been considered as a hedge against the possibility that leak rates in a high-pressure heavy water-cooled reactor would turn out to be too high. That has not happened.

In addition to travelling internationally to India and Argentina to supervise the low-power commissioning tests related to the physics characteristics of the reactors, I did a lot of international travel related to the marketing of CANDU 600 reactors abroad. This included attending technical meetings and conferences in the Netherlands, Italy, Spain, France, Turkey, Japan, and South Korea, in some cases more than once.

Helen joined me on my trip to Paris, which was of a short duration. Subsequently we went to Finland for a holiday to visit some of the Aspila family. Her mother was also there for a time and acted as our tour guide. My parents couldn't afford travel to Finland, so they hadn't maintained a connection with family there.

AECL was invited to send a reactor physics specialist to present lectures at a symposium on reactor physics methodology used for the CANDU reactor design. The symposium was organized by the International Institute of Theoretical Physics in Trieste, Italy. It was a week-long symposium.

My boss, Liberty Pease, asked me to prepare a series of lectures to deliver at the symposium. Having only been given short notice of the event, I was forced to dictate my lecture notes into a Dictaphone at home over the Christmas holidays.

Knowing that many of the attendees at this meeting would possess more advanced knowledge of mathematics and physics than myself, I prayed that I wouldn't be asked questions I couldn't answer.

Thankfully that didn't happen and I felt the symposium went well. The lectures were compiled in an AECL internal document which was used as a key training resource well after I retired.

When I returned to the office several years after retirement to attend a meeting, Ben Rouben, the reactor physics branch manager, said that they considered that document to be their bible.

DOMESTIC LIFE IN THE GREATER GTA

CHAPTER EIGHT

After living in an apartment for a short time, we learned of a unique townhouse development in the Jane and Finch area, the first condominium-type development in Canada. Condominium regulations hadn't been developed yet. We paid $12,000 for a townhouse with three bedrooms. We didn't own our unit, but we officially owned 1.5 percent of the complete village. It certainly was a big improvement over the apartment.

Our daughter Liisa was born in 1964 after we moved there. Two years later, our second daughter, Paivi-Lee, was born.

After the AECL power reactor design group moved to the Sheridan Park Research Centre in Mississauga, I started looking for a house not too far from the office. We moved into a spacious three-bedroom bungalow about two kilometres from the office.

In 1969, our son Paul was born. Around this time, my brother Albert also finished high school and joined the Air Force, becoming a navigator on sub-hunting aircrafts. My mother went to live with my half-sister Betty in Picton.

Once Paivi-Lee was born, Helen and I agreed to seek a church where we could get involved so our children could learn about Christianity as they grew up. Helen's parents had arranged for her to be confirmed by the Lutheran Church by correspondence, since there was no Finnish church in Deep River.

We found a local Lutheran church not too far from our home. Helen qualified for membership, but I first had to take instruction from the pastor on the doctrines of the church to qualify. He came to our home to teach me. This was the first time I had studied the Bible in depth, and two verses in the epistle to the Ephesians transformed my life: *"For it is by grace you have been saved, through faith—and this is not from yourselves, it is the gift of God—not by works, so that no one can boast"* (Ephesians 2:8–9).

Up to that point, I intellectually believed the Christmas and Easter stories but didn't have any assurance of my own salvation because I had believed I had to contribute to it through my performance. The Bible declared I had to be perfect in God's eyes to earn salvation, and I knew very well that I didn't measure up to this standard.

But the moment I read Ephesians 2:8–9, I received the gift of faith in Jesus from the Holy Spirit. I knew for sure that Jesus was my Saviour because through His crucifixion He had paid the price I could never pay due to the amazing grace of God for me. Ever since, I've had no fear of death because I know I will spend eternity in the presence of pure love. I also received Jesus Christ as the Lord of my life and have endeavoured to serve Him and build a relationship with Him through coming to know Him as revealed in the Holy Bible and communication in prayer.

About two years after Paul was born, Helen carried to full term our fourth child, a boy we named Lyal Peter, but he was stillborn. After Helen had been taken to the delivery room, I was told that Lyal would be stillborn because of his low brain function. I immediately phoned our pastor, David Kluge of the Lutheran Church, and he came to the hospital and prayed for me and Helen.

When I was allowed to go to Helen after the delivery, I was pleasantly surprised to see a smile on her face. She excitedly shared that Jesus had come into her room and assured her that He had come for Lyal.

A few days later, a member of my staff with whom we had become friends on a personal level came into my office and declared, "You and Helen are very good actors!" He had come with me the evening before to visit Helen in the hospital. We had been jovial in our conversation with him rather than conveying sadness or sorrow.

I asked him why he would say this and he explained that according to his belief system a tragedy like losing a child would be seen as a punishment for a terrible sin he had committed; because he wouldn't know what he had done that was so bad, he would be devastated.

I shared the reason for the joy within us and how he could have it, too. When you develop your relationship with God the Father, He demonstrates His love to you in such a way that it becomes an experience, a taste of love and security. In other words, you know without hesitation that God values you as His child. As 1 John 4:18 states, "*There is no fear in love. But perfect love drives out fear, because fear has to do with punishment. The one who fears is not made perfect in love.*" At this point in our spiritual walk with Christ Jesus, we had tasted the goodness, forgiveness, and friendship of a very loving Saviour God and so we weren't devastated by what had happened.

I served as the Sunday School superintendent and on the board of elders at Christ Our King Lutheran Church in Mississauga. I also helped with the evangelism outreach to the community.

In 1972, our pastor was asked by a representative from Gideons International to identify members in his congregation who had a heart for evangelism, and my name was mentioned. As a result of that, when I learned about the vision of the Gideons—to help ensure that as many people as possible received a copy of God's Word—I was excited, because of the way the Bible had transformed my life. My application was accepted, as well as Helen's, to join the Gideon Auxiliary and that has been my vocation ever since.

My most memorable experience as a Gideon volunteer occurred in Mississauga a few years after I joined. We had the privilege of offering Grade Five students in public school a small copy of the New Testament, along with Psalms and Proverbs. Around the time I joined, permission had been granted to do the same in separate schools as well. There was a Catholic Church and an associated separate school within walking distance from our home. I received permission from the priest to distribute the Testaments for the first time in their school.

When the time came, I was pleasantly surprised to find that they had planned a service in the church. All the children from Grade Four to Grade Eight come into the church and I was asked to give the homily, or sermon, as part of the program instead of the priest. As I passed out the Testaments to the children as they came forward in single file, the priest asked me to say to them, "This is the Word of God. It is light and life to you." I had seen many of these children grow up in the neighbourhood, so it was a great thrill to see their smiles as I gave them a copy of God's Word.

Helen and I supervised a youth group at our church and led a Bible study for them. Two of the group members, Lou Ann Young and Karen Hendriksen, later became missionaries in Africa and several others have kept in touch via Christmas cards. Lou Ann, the youth leader, was on fire for Jesus because she had received the spiritual gifts of the Holy Spirit in charismatic meetings in Toronto. Seeing the joy she reflected imparted a desire in us to connect with charismatic Christians. This took us in a new direction in our spiritual journey, resulting in many wonderful ministry experiences, some of which are recorded in a book Helen published.[16]

After Helen received Jesus as her Saviour in February 1968, her life became so transformed that she developed a goal in life to fulfill the purpose God had for her. This led her to begin studies and become an ordained minister. After her ordination, she worked in a large homecare centre doing chaplaincy work and going on very interesting missionary trips in Ontario. All were guided by the Holy Spirit and were very interesting, to say the least. It always amazes us when the Holy Spirit is in charge. We can clearly see the hand of God in these situations.

When our children were young, we usually spent our holidays camping in parks throughout Ontario or going to Deep River, Bruce Mines, Larder Lake, or Picton to visit relatives and our hometowns. I was blessed to have three weeks of holidays annually.

As the saying goes, you can take the boy or girl out of the country, but you can't take the country out of the boy or girl. We will always be country folks in our hearts! These family outings were very precious to me because of the opportunity to bond with our children. Helen and I are so grateful for the wonderful individuals all our children have turned out to be and the great blessing they are to us.

After Helen's father retired, his health deteriorated to the point where he couldn't do maintenance on their home. He also didn't like the idea of hiring others to do it for him, so he convinced his wife to sell the property in Deep River.

---

[16] Helen S. Pasanen, *Journey's to Unknown Spiritual Frontiers* (Winnipeg, MB: Word Alive Press, 2018).

We invited them to come and live with us in Mississauga. We hired a Finnish carpenter to partition our basement into two bedrooms for them, and the rec room served as a kitchen and dining room.

My father-in-law passed away a few years later, and after that we began to look for a rural property because we were drawn to the countryside. We purchased five acres northwest of Acton and planned to eventually build a house on it. In the spring and summer months, we often drove there on weekends to plant and tend to our small vegetable garden. A South Korean member of my branch at work also used part of this land for a time.

One day in early 1983, we noticed a For Sale sign on a country property about three kilometres north of Acton. It had a bungalow with three bedrooms on four acres of land. It had been split off from a one-hundred-acre farm. We fell in love with the property and moved there in November 1983. It had a pond which we excavated to make it larger. We were finally back in the country!

The previous owners of this property were an older couple. The man was a keen gardener and had planted virtually all the trees on the property. He'd planned it well so that banks of spruces and pines provided a great windbreak from the northwest winds in the winter.

The original farmer had used that land for grazing cattle, so it had been well-fertilized. When we moved there, the evergreens were fifteen to twenty feet tall, but they grew to about seventy feet in the thirty-four years we lived there. He had also purchased a mid-sized wheelhorse garden tractor with a five-foot mower and cultivator, with plough and snow blade attachments. When he realized we were also keen gardeners, he sold it to us for a good price. It was a great labour saver. We also brought the self-propelled rear-tine tiller we had bought in Mississauga. We used these aids to create two garden plots where we planted vegetables.

I continued working at AECL for eight years, so it was a busy but rewarding period for me. I am thankful that Helen also enjoyed the outdoor work, which lightened the load for me. She was quite an entrepreneur as well, running various small businesses from home, marketing various products such as air purifiers, health food supplements, and seaweed products for fertilizer and animal feed. She also worked as a sales agent for an RESP company.

Our oldest daughter Liisa had gone to Trent University, taking an education program. She has since worked as a teacher for many years and is currently the assistant pastor at her church. Paivi-Lee lived with us for a while, and Paul stayed for three years while he finished high school. Paul enrolled in the advertising program at Sheridan College after high school, and he has worked in advertising in Toronto since then. Paivi-Lee has held general administrative positions. She took necessary training to work for the Canadian National Institute for the Blind, and became an orientation specialist with them. She currently works for the federal government.

Before moving to the country, we joined a charismatic church in Etobicoke. We continued attending there several years after moving despite the long commute because we were being spiritually enriched by its teaching and practices. Helen and I participated in the evangelism outreach and other programs. I served on the board of elders and our son Paul was the drummer on the worship team. During the summers while attending Trent University, Liisa was hired as an assistant to one of the pastors.

We also continued to serve as Gideon volunteers. I served on the executive of the Halton Hills chapter and was responsible for the ministry in the town of Acton. We could no longer offer New Testaments to Grade Five students, but we offered them to children from the community attending summer kids camps. On a regular basis we looked for opportunities to offer the precious gift of God's word one-on-one in our daily interactions with people.

A Gideon isn't considered well-dressed unless he has a Scripture in his pocket. Early in 2016, a digital version of the complete Bible with helps was developed. Since then, we have been passing out free cards titled "Explore the Questions," which contains a QR code and web address that can be used to download a free app.[17] When circumstances permit, we share our testimony about the impact the Bible has had on our lives.

After Helen's father passed away, her mother wanted to be more independent. Eventually she ended up back in Deep River where she purchased a semidetached house in town. By this time, Deep River had become incorporated as a town and AECL no longer controlled who lived there. That turned out to be a blessing to me when I was appointed as liaison officer between CANDU Operations, CRNL, and the Whiteshell Nuclear Laboratories near Winnipeg, Manitoba. The Whiteshell facility was established by AECL primarily to design and build a small research reactor to test the feasibility of building a nuclear power reactor based on using an organic liquid as a coolant.

Teams of specialists in various disciplines worked at all three sites to develop analytical software using experimental data. My job as liaison officer was to enhance communication between these teams to avoid unnecessary duplication. I spent the majority of my time at Deep River, so I was glad to be able to stay with my mother-in-law. The negative side of this was the extra workload Helen had to carry when I was away. Fortunately, it was a relatively short-term assignment of two years. I'm sure Helen thought that was plenty.

When we realized Helen's mother was developing health issues that compromised her ability to live alone, we looked for

---

17   The address is www.newlife.bible.

a way to have her come to live with us while maintaining a degree of independence. Our bungalow in Erin had a two-car garage that was accessible from our kitchen. We thought it was big enough to convert into a small apartment, so we hired a renovation contractor to convert the garage into a three-room legal apartment and built a separate oversized two-car garage about fifty feet from the house. My mother-in-law sold her house in Deep River and came to live in the apartment.

After returning home, I worked again as manager of the Reactor Physics Branch for about three and one half years. The peak of the CANDU reactor design work by AECL had reached a climax before I was appointed liaison officer, so the CANDU design group had to be downsized. The two physics branches were collapsed into one. The only new design project was a 300-megawatt CANDU-type reactor which was unsuccessfully marketed primarily in the U.S.

Although the design work diminished, the international marketing work continued. In 1990, I was part of a team sent to the Netherlands. It was an intense week, and when I returned home Helen understandably asked me to take her out for dinner. I had to tell her I could not, because I had a lot of work to do since I had to deliver a report the next morning.

In the morning, I got up early, had my breakfast, and took a walk around our property as usual. I had a cough, and as I walked I experienced some chest pains which I associated with the cough. That morning at work, I experienced some more chest pains. Thankfully, it happened to be a day when we had a nurse on site and I decided to talk to her about it.

She checked me out and urged me to go to the hospital to have my heart function checked. At the hospital, an internal medicine specialist gave me an ECG and then put me on a treadmill. I didn't have chest pains on the treadmill, but I tired quickly.

While resting after getting off the treadmill, Helen showed up. She had been notified that I was going to the Credit Valley Hospital. She didn't think I looked well at all. However, the doctor didn't see any reason why I couldn't go home. He gave me nitro-glycerine and instructed me to take it if I had pain. If the pain persisted after taking it repeatedly, I should come back.

A few minutes after leaving, I had some pain. Helen took one look at me, turned around, and took me back to the emergency department. They found that my blood pressure had dropped and admitted me immediately. The bloodwork verified that I had experienced a heart attack, which resulted in me requiring a triple bypass operation. I know it wasn't a coincidence that the nurse, Alice Wilberforce, had been on duty at my office that particular day.

When I returned to work in about one month, I realized that stress had probably been a big contributor to my health problems. I found managing a large physics branch quite stressful and asked my boss if there was another less demanding role available for me.

I was then appointed to serve as manager of the Licensing and Risk Assessment Branch, which had a smaller group of people. My main activity in this role was preparing documentation in support of the licensability of the CANDU 300 design in the U.S. I travelled to the U.S. several times in connection with this job to attend meetings. I also presented a paper in San Francisco at a American Nuclear Society meeting for which I was given a certificate of recognition.

During the summer of 1991, the company announced a financial incentive program to encourage employees nearing retirement age to opt for early retirement. This was all part of the necessity to downsize further with most of the projects nearing completion. I wasn't very close to nominal retirement age of sixty-five, but I had completed thirty-four years of service to the company and was just one year short of qualifying for the maximum pension.

After discussing the situation with Helen, we decided to seize the opportunity. In August I found myself having gone full circle from splitting atoms to splitting wood again. We had a woodburning stove in our home in Erin and didn't have to purchase any firewood while we lived there. Management of the forest on our property yielded everything we needed. In fact, we were able to give away a lot of firewood to needy families. Surplus food from the garden was given to the food bank in Acton.

LIFE ON OUR
GREEN ACRES

CHAPTER NINE

It's interesting that my last day of employment with AECL co-
incided with a prearranged meeting with Gordon Upton, editor and executive director of the Pentecostal Assemblies of Canada. His office wasn't far from where my office had been.

Helen and I had met him when we were attending a Pentecostal Church in Erin. He had been the guest speaker one Sunday
and we took him out for lunch. At that time, he'd been the editor
of an evangelism tract called *Real Living* published by National
Men's Fellowship Ministries. He would look for stories of interesting people who were committed Christians and willing to have
their testimony published. At that meeting, he'd said that he would
like to interview me as a possible subject for their next publication.

Following his interview with me, a publication titled *Escap-
ing the Final Meltdown* was issued. It was a sixteen-page booklet in
which the consequences of the Chernobyl reactor accident were
described in some detail. It also mentioned the role my branch
had played in simulating the reactor conditions leading up to the
accident, which proved that the operators had permitted the reactor to get into a very abnormal operating condition that effectively
rendered ineffective the shutdown system that would normally

have shut the reactor down. The result was a steam explosion and the graphite moderator was set on fire. The operators were found to have violated six operating policies related to safety, in the process of allowing the reactor to continue operating under unsafe conditions. The severe damage done to the facility and other consequences are well known. The booklet also provides a brief description of the CANDU design, explaining that the Chernobyl accident could not occur with a CANDU reactor.

The article also summarized my spiritual journey. When Upton asked me about my faith as a nuclear scientist, I responded, "To me, Christ is the answer. I have absolutely no question about the reason why He came. He is the way God chose to communicate the way of salvation. He is the message of God to mankind for our daily lives and also the answer for eternal life." After twenty-nine years, I remain absolutely convinced of that.

The booklet also explains Helen's role in praying for the Mississauga train derailment that occurred in 1979. This is described in her book, *Journeys to Unknown Spiritual Frontiers*.[18]

A number of complimentary copies were given to me to use in our witnessing. As a Gideon volunteer, we have the opportunity to offer copies of the New Testament with Psalms and Proverbs to people who are hungry to get to know the God who changed our lives. We received permission from the Pentecostal Association of Canada to make a few hundred copies of the tract to hand out with the Gideon Bibles.

An unusual method soon opened for me to use this tract to witness indirectly to some of my former colleagues from work. I was invited to participate on two AECL committees after I retired. One dealt with how we could counteract the anti-nuclear sentiments in society, including the church. I mentioned that

[18]   Helen S. Pasanen, *Journey's to Unknown Spiritual Frontiers* (Winnipeg, MB: Word Alive Press, 2018).

nuclear had been given a positive spin in the Pentecostal tract. The chairman took a copy of the tract and included a copy of it in the minutes of the meeting.

Several of my colleagues chose to continue working in the nuclear field for a number of years. After retirement from AECL, some worked as consultants to the utilities that owned nuclear reactors, while others took teaching positions at universities.

One of my senior staff members took a position with the Federal Nuclear Regulatory Organization in Ottawa a few years before I retired. It was called the Atomic Energy Control Board. At the time of my retirement, he was looking for outside help to deliver a course on reactor physics to groups of trainees from nuclear regulation agencies in Indonesia and Romania. Knowing I had retired, he gave me the contract to deliver the courses. The course material had been prepared, so I didn't have to do much preparation. I made two trips to Ottawa to deliver the courses.

That was the last work I did in the field, outside of serving on committees back at Sheridan Park. However, to keep informed I have retained membership in the Canadian Nuclear Society, which I have held since its inception. I held some executive positions in it while I was still working and was instrumental in establishing the annual Simulation Symposium, where papers on computer modelling software developed for power reactor design are presented. I am pleased to see that it is still being held.

During retirement, it was a joy and a blessing to be able to be immersed in God's creation all day rather than only in the evenings and on weekends. We had quite a long bucket list of projects built up, so I certainly didn't find myself with nothing to do.

Interestingly, another health issue I had to deal with in my last few years of work was trigeminal neuralgia. I frequently had severe attacks of pain in the nerves on my face. Helen said that my face became distorted when an attack occurred. The doctor said it would be risky to operate and so he prescribed a drug which had, as one side effect, death. It wasn't effective. Homeopathic remedies eventually reduced the frequency of the attacks somewhat. I haven't had a single attack since I retired, which would indicate that the malady was also triggered by stress.

About three years after I retired, Helen's mother Hilda passed away. She had lived with us for six years. Shortly thereafter, I heard from my Aunt Hilda that she had developed wet macular degeneration to the point where she could no longer drive her car. She had moved to Texas to help a relative of her husband, who had passed away at a young age from a heart attack in the late 1950s. The relative she cared for had also passed away and now she was renting a small guest house in the country. She needed to find a place to live that was much closer to shopping and healthcare facilities.

Knowing that she needed someone to help her, I flew down to Corpus Christie, Texas. Before leaving, I discussed with Helen the possibility of offering Hilda the option of coming back with me to live in our apartment since it was now vacant. She was eighty-four years old, so we didn't expect it would be a long-term proposition. Helen agreed to the idea.

In talking it over with Hilda, she shared with me that she had been encouraged by people from her church to go on a waiting list for a Lutheran assisted living facility. The problem with this was the fact that she would have to entrust someone to look after her affairs when she could no longer handle them. This would raise the possibility of her being taken advantage of by people we didn't know. In the end, she accepted the idea of coming home with me.

It took two weeks to put all her affairs in order before we could drive back to Erin in her car. I rented a mid-sized trailer because she wanted to take some furniture with her, as well as her cat.

It took four days of driving to make the trip, and I was concerned what we would face trouble at the border. Fortunately, we were blessed and the border official only asked me to open the back door of the trailer; he took a quick look and allowed us to proceed into Canada.

For most of the fourteen years Hilda lived in our apartment her restricted vision didn't prohibit her from taking care of herself domestically, including cooking. However, her health issues, including atrial fibrillation, did demand quite a bit of my time. I also helped a lot with her financial affairs. I am thankful to have had this opportunity to give back to her because of the sacrifices she had to make to set me on my career.

In her late nineties, Hilda began to show symptoms of dementia which made it more challenging to care for her. Fortunately, we found a respite centre where she was willing to go for two weeks periodically to give us a break from this stress. During a longer respite period, we had a contractor build an addition onto the apartment which significantly increased the space. When I brought Hilda home, she didn't even notice it had been done. When I explained what we'd done, she just said, "I don't need this extra space!"

After her ninety-seventh birthday, Hilda's dementia had developed to the point where it became difficult to handle. We decided it was time to look for a nursing home in the U.S., since she was an American citizen. Hilda had a nephew living in Niagara Falls whose son, Dan, advised us to talk to an American lawyer he knew (being a lawyer himself) about how to get Hilda on a waiting list for nursing homes in the area. This was clearly God-ordained, because this lawyer turned out to be a board member for a Catholic nursing home in Lewiston, New York. He managed to pull strings and I soon received a phone call from the nursing home explaining that I could bring Hilda there in two weeks! It was a very convenient location to visit, since there was a bridge from Canada that crossed directly into Lewiston.

I was concerned about taking Hilda back to the U.S., because the only identification she had was her birth certificate, which was printed on parchment paper and didn't have a photo.[19] This was after 9/11, so photo ID was mandatory at the border.

Helen had chosen a personalized license plate for our van which read IM4GOD. The first thing the U.S. border official said as we drove up was, "I really like your license plate!" I showed him Hilda's birth certificate and explained that I was bringing her to a nursing home in Lewiston. He took a look at her and said, "Go ahead."

It was a very caring nursing home and Hilda seemed happy there. She passed away less than a year later. My cousin and I were joint executors for her will and I was very grateful for the great help his son Dan gave us in the process.

We continued living on our wonderful four acres for many years. The property had the added blessing of it being the choice location for family gatherings on special occasions like Christmas, Easter, Thanksgiving, Father's and Mother's Day, and sometimes for birthdays. Two of our children lived within a short driving distance from us and the third one also lived nearby for stretches of time. The grandkids enjoyed many outdoor activities because the property was a hilly lot for tobogganing. We also had a pond for skating in winter, and we had a good time checking out all the life in it during the summer. I have many fond memories of these times.

At Christmas, we agreed that each person would only receive one gift, so it fell on me to draw names. No one would have

---

[19] She had been born in the U.S., as had my own mother. My grandfather had moved around a lot to find work. In those days, free movement between Canada and the U.S. had been allowed.

to buy gifts for another member of their immediate family, and we defined a limit on the cost of the gift and asked each person to provide a list of suggestions.

At Easter, weather permitting, I would devise an egg hunt outdoors. Of course, I also gave them clues to make it feasible to find them all on four acres of land. It was a challenge to think of something new each time, but the children apparently looked forward to see what Grandpa Art came up with every year.

Another thing I did for the grandkids was build a six-by-eight raised garden for each of them so they could plant their own vegetables each spring and harvest the crop in the fall. The idea was to stir up in them an interest in gardening. Of course, that meant we had to water and weed their gardens as well as ours. We had a pump installed at the pond to make watering very convenient.

Our two granddaughters Ava and Bronte Pasanen, were so excited about growing carrots that they set up a booth in front of their house in Toronto to sell their produce. In fact, the eldest, Ava, enjoyed playing a farmer on the internet in which she grew crops and sold them, buying more land with her profits.

Our granddaughter Laura's daughter Erica, who was near Bronte's age, also participated in these activities, and our grandson Michael Farrugia enjoyed operating our power equipment when he was older. We eventually traded in our wheelhorse tractor for a smaller John Deere that didn't have the gardening attachments. The rear-tine tiller we had purchased to use in the garden in our lot northwest of Acton before moving to Erin was adequate. We used the tiller for thirty-seven years, partly because Helen rebuilt it as part of a small engines course she took. We also had a walk-behind snowblower in addition to the tractor attachment.

The following is intended to provide a brief picture of what occupied my time in the many years I was blessed to live in the country after retirement from AECL.

In the winter, I split and hauled wood from our woodshed to keep our woodburning stove going. I didn't have to split wood for kindling because we would use the wood that we'd pruned from our five apple trees in early spring. These were placed in boxes and they would be dry enough by winter to use. Helen helped me with that, as well as clearing snow from the long driveway and pathways to the woodshed, indoor maintenance on the house, and catching up on paperwork and doing forest management.

In the spring, I pruned apple trees and raspberry bushes and planted seeds in the garden at the appropriate time. We would start frost-sensitive plants under lamps indoors. I also cleaned the leaves that were left over from the fall, fertilized the gardens with kelp powder and other natural fertilizers, cut the grass with a push mower where Helen couldn't get to it with the tractor, tilled the gardens when the weather permitted, managed the forest, removed anti-freeze and primed the pond pump and installed the aerator, and planted annual flowers, And of course I helped prepare for family get-togethers.

During the summer, I weeded and watered the vegetable gardens and harvested some crops. I also managed the lawn and flowerbeds with Helen and took care of the forest, including harvesting firewood from dead and storm damaged trees.

In the fall, I harvested crops and prepared them for storage in our crawl space in the basement. It was insulated just enough to keep them all winter.[20] If we had a surplus of food, we would donate it to the food bank. We also raked a lot of leaves and stacked them to compost for the gardens, as well as hauled manure from a nearby sheep farmer in our four-by-eight trailer and spread it on the gardens. The farmer was a friend who worked with me as a volunteer Gideon. I also winterized the pond pump and removed the aerator, prepared for our Christmas family

---

[20]   This includes squash, beets, carrots, parsnips, potatoes, onions, and apples.

get-togethers, and did forest management. Forest management was a particular challenge in 2013 when a severe ice storm caused a lot of tree damage.

There was also much work to do year-round. Caregiving, church activities, and volunteer work for the Gideons demanded quite a lot of my time. A daily activity involved walking one or two of our rescue dogs.

In my late seventies, my physical activities became quite restricted because of arthritic pain in my hips. Fortunately, it didn't occur simultaneously. Instead of hip replacements, I opted for shockwave therapy at a clinic in Kitchener. It was a slow process but resulted in greatly improved mobility. However, as time went on it became increasingly difficult to do the physical work at the same level, especially forest management. We hired men from our church to do the woodwork and we also allowed them to use two of our garden plots.

After the ice storm of 2013, Liisa and Peter Farrugia pleasantly surprised us by bringing a team of people from her church in Brantford to spend a day helping us clean up. What a blessing! Helen and I continued working on the clean-up for about a year, with help from family members when they came to visit. That's how long it took to return to normal.

Another special blessing occurred when our son-in-law, David Wilson, and our granddaughter Laura built a nice screened gazebo for us overlooking the pond one summer when Helen and I were on vacation for two weeks. We enjoyed having our meals there in the summer.

I suffered a huge setback in my late seventies when I fell and fractured my left femur. I had missed the bottom step on a stepping stool in the basement while dismounting and fell backwards. Fortunately, the fracture occurred at a location which permitted a pin to be inserted so my functionality wasn't impaired too much. I was also diagnosed with prostate cancer. Hormone therapy and taking supplements suggested by a naturopathic oncologist has kept it under control—along with prayer, of course.

Early in 2016, our health circumstances were such that we agreed the time had come to give up the country property we had enjoyed for thirty-four years. Because our two daughters both lived in Brantford at the time, our idea was to rent an apartment in a seniors centre which also contained an assisted living facility and a long-term care centre. We had visited three such facilities a year earlier and were put on their waiting lists.

We decided to work with a zero-commission real estate agency to sell our property, for a fee of $3,000. They advertised the property online and also provided limited legal services. After the initial meeting with their representative, all communication with them and their legal team occurred by email. They hired a firm that uses drones to take the photos for advertising and produced brochures that were placed in a rack at the end of our driveway. We thought their promotion was superior to what any real estate agent had done for us in earlier cases. It was our responsibility to show the property to perspective buyers.

The timing was clearly ordained by God because the day after the listing went online, we showed the property to two parties and the second one ended up making an offer at the asking price. He and his wife had been looking all day for a smaller country property than the one they already owned, and that's when they saw our sign on their way home. We hadn't yet heard of any vacancies in the senior centres we'd applied to, but Paivi-Lee and her husband David agreed we could live with them until we found an apartment.

The day after we received a firm offer on our property, we received a call from Paivi-Lee. She told us that she had been hired to work for the federal government—in Edmonton. So they would be moving two weeks after the closing date on our property. After meeting with them, it was decided that we would buy their house. It was a split-entrance, three-bedroom bungalow on a small city lot. We felt we could easily manage the maintenance work required.

A characteristic of Finnish *sisu* is a waste-not-want-not attitude. An example of this can be seen in the fact that I wanted to move the remaining cedar lumber from a portable sauna we had installed under our front veranda of our Mississauga house to Brantford. I had disassembled it so it could be moved to our home in Erin. We'd used it as a sauna in our basement for several years but eventually removed it to provide more space. We had a drive-through shed built near the house for which I constructed four doors from that cedar. I also built two doors for a woodshed. There was now enough material left over to build three planters and a raised vegetable garden in Brantford.

It wasn't long after moving that we hired a landscaper who attended our daughter's church to convert the backyard into three small vegetable gardens. This helped alleviate the adjustment we needed to make in going back to city living. In regard to the Gideon ministry, I had expected to find a thriving chapter in Brantford, but instead I was shocked to find only one member who was eighty-six and severely limited by poor health. He passed away two years after we arrived. I believe this was another reason we were meant to move. Helen and I worked together to rejuvenate the Gideon ministry in Brantford.

For the first two years, we were kept very busy. Our task was to connect with as many pastors of Christian churches in Brantford and Paris as possible to share with them the vision of the Gideons and the many new scripture resources that had been developed. As a result, many churches are now cooperating with us in our fundraising programs.

We've also had many opportunities to distribute New Testaments and magazines to children at vacation Bible schools, sports camps, Grade Five students in Christian schools, and those who attend annual kids camps. The distribution to students in public schools and separate schools has been prohibited for many years. Instead of using Scriptures in book form to offer people I interact with on a daily basis, I now offer a card with a QR code for a free app. Feedback has always been positive. Scripture magazines called *Hope* have also been placed with permission in waiting rooms at many healthcare centres.

SUMMING UP

CHAPTER TEN

Perhaps the best way to sum up this brief retrospective of my eighty-five-plus years of life is to highlight those aspects which have been most impactful in my personal development as well as the life lessons I have received. To put some order to it, I'll categorize according to the duration of the topic in my life.

The grace of God. The common thread throughout my life is being a recipient of God's grace. Grace is defined as undeserved love. In looking back, I know that my steps have been ordered by the Lord as promised in the Bible.

Fifty-eight years of marriage. Unquestionably, the marriage to my beautiful blond bomber was ordained in heaven. Helen has impacted my personal development in a multitude of ways. She has been my loving, devoted wife, best friend, partner, and counsellor for my body, soul, and spirit, for which I will be eternally grateful. She has been my health consultant, spiritual motivator, and the greatest gift God has given me, second only to the gift of faith in Jesus Christ.

Helen has always embraced family values, reflected in the way she has parented our three wonderful children with love, kindness, generosity, and spiritual counselling and discernment.

Too many times she has had to fill the role of a single parent because of my obligations while I worked for AECL.

She did all of this while fulfilling the call on her life to serve the Lord as an ordained prophetic intercessor. This required learning Scripture, reading the many books in our extensive library, and completing many courses on counselling both in-class and by correspondence. She also authored many inspirational booklets and a daily devotional. In her later years, she published three books, all the while managing a small business and serving as our family's financial manager and cook.

One of Helen's favourite choruses is based on 2 Timothy 1:12, which says, *"I know whom I have believed, and am convinced that he is able to guard what I have entrusted to him until that day."* In fact, the preceding verses are a great expression of the faith that has motivated Helen in all aspects of her life.

All this to explain why I am so blessed and thankful that God brought us together, even if it meant colliding in a grocery store! I am also very thankful for the blessing that our three children and their spouses have been to me through their love and support in many ways.

Thirty-four years in the Canadian nuclear power industry. Perhaps the greatest impact on my personal development from my work at AECL is that the experience has demonstrated the validity of the promises in Scripture for one who has come into a relationship with Jesus Christ through faith.

As an example, Psalm 32:8 says *"I will instruct you and teach you in the way you should go; I will counsel you with my loving eye on you."* I believe that the story of my life's journey is a testimony of a fulfillment of that promise.

Consider the fact that an introverted boy of seventeen, who felt so inadequate to speak to a group of parents as valedictorian that it made him too sick to do it, was taken on a track in which he was asked to deliver seven lectures on CANDU nuclear design at the Winter College on Nuclear Physics and Reactors organized by the International Institute of Theoretical Physics in Trieste, Italy. I was entrusted by my boss to do this on short notice, which forced me to dictate the associated report of 157 pages at home during the Christmas holidays.[21] I didn't inherently have the aptitude to accomplish this, but God gave me the courage and resilience to accept the challenge. He gave me what I needed to accomplish it.

I believe that, because we are created in the image of God, we are born with a free will. He has a destiny for each of us and orchestrates circumstances in our lives through which we are given choices to make. We have to make the right choices to achieve the destiny He has for us.

Looking back, it's clear that many of the choices I made along the journey resulted in positive outcomes. The ones that did not served as life lessons for me.

It's interesting that a new translation of the New Testament which we recently acquired, called *The Pure Word*,[22] very frequently adds the words "by your choice" when we are told what we should be doing to live a life pleasing to God. This translation was produced over a period of twenty years by a group of scholars whose task was to convert the original text into English as literally as possible without interpretation to make it more understandable.

There are some who would question whether spending thirty-four years contributing to development of the CANDU nuclear power reactors is a "positive outcome." My position on this is that

---

[21]   This was at a time in history when documents were still produced by a secretary from a Dictaphone. I am so thankful for Irene Winter facing the challenge of typing it from the Dictaphone in a short time.

[22]   *The Pure Word: The Complete New Testament From Matthew through Revelation* (Henderson, NV: One Path Publishing, 2018).

God provided sufficient resources on planet Earth to be utilized to sustain mankind and other life for as long as He has ordained. He also created us with the intellectual ability and curiosity to discover how those resources should be employed. That is why uranium fission was discovered experimentally before it was realized that the process had occurred naturally at some point in the past.

Here's a summary of the positives of nuclear power.

First, nuclear power is cleaner than solar power. Like solar power, a nuclear plant emits zero greenhouse gases while generating electricity. When the lifecycle of energy sources is taken into account, nuclear is cleaner. Lifecycle analysis accounts for emissions from cradle-to-grave, taking into account actions involved in the initial build to the last actions taken to dismantle it. The construction of both nuclear and solar plants require energy that comes from fossil fuels, and the same is true when a plant is closed, dismantled, and the waste disposed of. An intergovernmental panel on climate change confirmed that nuclear energy produces less greenhouse gases than solar power per kilowatt hour of electricity produced. Wind energy produces slightly lower greenhouse gases than nuclear and hydroelectric power is the lowest.

Second, nuclear power is important when it comes to the issue of climate change. The CANDU program has replaced all electricity production in Ontario by coal-burning power plants and minimized the production by natural gas. Burning fossil fuels emits a great deal of carbon dioxide into the atmosphere, which contributes to climate change. A detailed study published by Kharecha and Hansen in 2013[23] indicates that electricity

---

[23] Pushker A. Kharecha and James E. Hansen, *Prevented Mortality and Greenhouse Gas Emissions from Historical and Projected Nuclear Power*. March 15, 2013 (https://pubs.acs.org/doi/10.1021/es3051197). Note that permission was granted by ACS Publications to reuse the material I excerpted from this article. Readers need further permission to reuse that or other material from this article in another publication.

production by nuclear energy in the world during the period between 1971 and 2009 prevented the release of sixty-four billion tonnes of greenhouse gases. CANDU reactors in Ontario prevent forty-five million tonnes of CO_2 per year.

Third, nuclear power saves lives. Fossil fuels emit sulphur oxides and nitrogen oxides. These pollutants worsen respiratory illnesses and cause death. In their report, Kharecha and Hansen estimated that world nuclear energy, by displacing fossil-fuelled electrical generation, resulting in the prevention of 1.84 million air-pollution-related deaths from 1971 to 2009. As an example of this, Ontario completed the switchover from coal to nuclear in 2014. Smog advisories and smog days dropped to zero in 2014 and 2015.

Four, medical radioisotopes produced in nuclear reactors in Canada have saved and extended millions of lives. The Pickering and Bruce reactors have produced cobalt-60 for many years. They account for seventy percent of the world's supply of cobalt-60.

The Pickering reactors have been producing cobalt-60 since the beginning. Dr. John Brenciaglia of Ontario Hydro and I were instrumental in proposing that the control rods that are in the core during normal operation be changed from steel to cobalt, so that cobalt-60 could be produced. Ontario Hydro agreed with the idea. John and I interacted a lot to establish a fair price for the cobalt-60.

I have been encouraged to learn recently that production of other isotopes is planned for the Bruce and Darlington reactors. Molybdenum-99 will be produced at Darlington, as it has been for some time in the Bruce reactors and in NRU for most of its lifetime. Considerations are underway to produce two other isotopes as well. One of these is effective in treating prostate cancer.

The unique design of CANDU reactors permits this. The use of pressure tubes and on-power fuelling makes it possible to dedicate a fuel channel to this purpose, allowing a lot of flexibility in controlling the irradiation time without having to shut down the reactor. This is not possible in PWR and BWR reactors, which dominate world nuclear electricity production, because they require refuelling off-power. Longer half-life isotopes like cobalt-60 can be produced in control rods that do require a reactor shutdown to harvest the isotope.

And finally, the life of these reactors can be extended by refurbishment. The pressure tube design unique to CANDU reactors makes refurbishment both possible and economic to extend the lifetime of the plants. In fact, refurbishment is currently underway in most of the CANDU plants around the world, extending their lifetime by many decades.

Twenty-nine years in retirement. The choice to take an early retirement also led to a positive result from my point of view. Atomic Energy of Canada is a crown corporation, which meant I received the same pension and insurance benefits as a federal employee. Because our three adult children were no longer dependents, we could continue to live on our country property comfortably with a thirty-two percent reduction in my income.

When most farmers are asked why they farm, they say it's for the sheer love of the land and livestock. I can fully understand that sentiment, having lived on and cared for a country property for thirty-four years, especially the twenty-five years when I didn't have any career obligations.

When our daughter Liisa was in public school at the age of twelve, she created a picture of me in coveralls holding a pitchfork with the words "One is closer to God in the garden than anyplace else on earth." Helen and I can certainly attest to that. Genesis 2:15 tells us that God placed the first human in the garden to work it and take care of it. There's no question that spiritual enrichment comes from spending time in the garden. Even

Jesus would go to a garden or mountain to pray. Farming and agriculture were man's first assignment from the Creator and it has remained a most noble and essential profession.

Retirement also freed me to contribute more to the Gideon ministry as a volunteer, which continues to be my vocation. I have found it spiritually enriching to work with committed groups of men and women from various Christian denominations in the Halton Hills chapter as well as with the pastors of Acton churches. I've also had time to assist with a major renovation of a church, build infrastructure for a Salvation Army thrift store, take shifts for the Christmas Kettle Program, and work with Helen on her mission trips to northern Ontario.

After moving to Brantford in 2016, Helen and I have continued to serve as Gideon volunteers in the Brantford chapter.

A Look Ahead

As I was writing these memoirs, I received news about future developments in energy supply that I find exciting and encouraging. Increasingly, there is talk about the "hydrogen economy" and small modular reactors (SMRs).

When I first heard about development of fuel cell technology many years ago, I envisioned an ideal future world in which electricity production by burning fossil fuels would be replaced by one in which electricity produced by nuclear fission was used to separate hydrogen from oxygen in water using electrolysis. The hydrogen acts like a carrier of the energy used to produce it when used in a fuel cell to be converted back to electrical energy. The only emission from this process is water. Nuclear energy is not only emissions free but also consumes far fewer natural resources per unit of energy produced.[24]

Firms like Ballard Power Systems[25] and Hydrogenics[26] were pioneers in fuel cell development beginning about twenty years ago. They have found lucrative markets outside of Canada and U.S. Fuel cell technology powers thousands of buses and heavy trucks around the world. A Vancouver-based company, Loop Energy, which has been in business for nineteen years, secured its first sale of its hydrogen fuel cell range extenders for short- and long-haul trucks in China last year. It has since sold a minority stake in its company to Cummins, a global manufacturer of diesel and alterative engine drive trains. Volkswagen and Alstrom are also investing in hydrogen drive-train components for buses, trucks, and trains.

The International Economic Forum in 2017 at Davos set the following target for fuel cell electric vehicles (FCEVs) by 2030: 350,000 commercial trucks, 50,000 buses, thousands of trains and ships, and one in twelve cars sold in California, Germany, Japan, and South Korea.

The Government of Canada has established a Hydrogen Strategy Steering Committee. The Canadian Nuclear Association has submitted a number of recommendations to the committee, including the following: "the government adopt fiscal and policy measures to support the development of SMR's which have the potential to generate the vast amounts of emissions— free hydrogen needed for a successful hydrogen economy."[27]

---

[24] The energy density of nuclear reactor fuel is a million times higher than the energy density of coal.

[25] www.ballard.com

[26] www.hydrogenics.com

[27] Taken from a CNA notification with permission from the CNA communications department.

Ontario Power Generation's Darlington Station is the only site in Ontario already licensed for additional reactors and they have proposed to build the first SMR in Ontario. Bruce County, where the Bruce nuclear facility is located, saw a recent announcement by the Saugeen First Nation. On December 7, 2020, they said that Hatch Ltd. And Plan Group Inc. had been selected to support the foundational work required to advance the Bruce foundational hydrogen infrastructure project, with the intent of transforming the Bruce region into Canada's clean energy capital. Off-peak surplus electricity from the Bruce reactors are to be used to produce hydrogen by electrolysis. The region is endowed with underground geologic formations in which vast amounts of hydrogen can be stored.

A huge advantage of FCEVs over battery-powered electric vehicles is that fuel cells have virtually zero waste. Ballard has demonstrated that they can reclaim ninety-five percent of the fuel cell stack so that far fewer toxic chemicals and waste products end up in landfills than is the case for batteries.

So what are SMRs? Small modular reactors produce energy from nuclear fission. They are emissions-free energy sources that can be practically built in a wide variety of locations around the world, such as remote communities in the far north that rely on diesel generators.

There is a rapidly growing interest in SMRs around the world. A number of different designs are being proposed. In October 2020, Canada's Minister of Innovation, Science and Industry announced a $20 million investment in Terrestrial Energy to support development of its integral molten salt reactor (IMSR). Terrestrial Energy is a company in Oakville, Ontario that was established by former AECL employees, at least two of whom I worked with. The IMSR uses a eutectic fluoride with low-enriched uranium fuel (UF4) which remains in liquid form at 600 to 700 degrees Celsius at atmospheric pressure. This means it can support many industrial process heat applications, like desalination and producing electricity efficiently. The moderator is graphite and the capacity is 195 megawatts. The federal Minister of Natural Resources announced in December 18, 2020 that SMR development is part of Canada's plan to reduce emissions to zero by 2050.

The U.S. National Regulatory Commission has already approved the first SMR design in the U.S. It's called NuScale and its capacity is only 50 megawatts, but many can be built at the same site. They are also evaluating the IMSR for licensing in the U.S.

So does this mean the CANDU design is obsolete? Not at all. In 2016, SNC Lavalin signed an agreement in principle for a joint venture with China National Nuclear Corporation and Shanghai Electric Company for the commercial development of the advanced fuel CANDU reactor (AFCR). This was a significant milestone for the CANDU product because it marks the first time an advanced fuel cycle will be developed for commercial application in CANDU while paving the way for more use of advanced fuels.

CANDU is the most flexible commercial platform for advanced fuels in operation today. A staff member of my branch, Adi Dastur, did the physics analysis which showed that spent fuel from LWRs and BWRs (water-cooled reactors) could be used as fuel for a CANDU without reprocessing. Since China and South Korea have both LWRs and CANDUs, they can reduce resource consumption by using AFCRs. China in particular expects it could use a combination of AFCRs and LWRs to develop a closed fuel cycle within the country, because analysis has shown that thorium could also be used in AFCRs, which is abundant in China. Thorium is considered a "breeder" fuel. Natural thorium (Th232) has no fissile isotopes, but fissile U233 is produced in thorium that is combined in reactor fuel with U235 and/or fissile plutonium. This is the result of neutrons being captured by thorium atoms.

These developments point to the fact that a huge reduction in world carbon dioxide emissions and other environmental benefits is possible if the large-scale adoption of the hydrogen economy occurs, combined with nuclear fission as the energy source. Of course, I won't see this happen on earth before graduating to my eternal home, but I am happy to see the pieces start to come together.

I am so thankful to have progressed from splitting wood to splitting atoms for thirty-four years, but the following twenty-nine years was back to splitting wood and sharing the good news. This has also been a great blessing from God for me. It is undoubtedly a huge factor in maintaining my health.

In regard to my vocation, I will continue serving the Brantford chapter of Gideons International in Canada as long as I am able, because of the great importance of people learning of the good news conveyed in the Bible. The gospels of Matthew, Mark, Luke, and John are biographies of the life of Jesus Christ on earth. The authors lived during the period when Jesus was on the earth, and two of them were His apostles. They were eyewitnesses and participants in most of His activities, validating His divinity.

The Apostle John wrote, "*That which was from the beginning, which we have heard, which we have seen with our eyes, which we have looked at and our hands have touched—this we proclaim concerning the Word of life*" (1 John 1:1). He also wrote, "*Jesus performed many other signs in the presence of his disciples, which are not recorded in this book. But these are written that you may believe that Jesus is the Messiah, the Son of God, and that by believing you may have life in his name*" (John 20:30–31).

I have no doubt that God's plan from the beginning of creation was to come to earth in the person of Jesus Christ to communicate to us how we can live our daily lives filled with peace and joy, recognizing the purpose He has for us, and most of all provide the answer to the sin question on the cross by His amazing grace.

The words of Scripture are the primary means used by the Holy Spirit to impart the gift of faith in our hearts and give us spiritual rebirth. Helen and I have found the Bible to be a God-given map for our spiritual journey. Whether we realize it or not, from the moment we are born we are placed on a spiritual journey. When we are old enough to ask questions, we begin to seek answers to life's deepest puzzles. Why are we here on earth? Is there a God? How do I know right from wrong? What happens when I die? Science does not provide answers to these questions.

APPENDIX

ARTHUR PASANEN'S RESUMÉ

Education

+ 1956 B.S.E. (Engineering Mechanics), University of Michigan, Ann Arbor, Michigan, United States.
+ 1956 B.S.E. (Engineering Mathematics), University of Michigan, Ann Arbor, Michigan United States.
+ 1957 M.S.E. (Nuclear Engineering), University of Michigan, Ann Arbor, Michigan, United States.

Experience

+ Manager, Licensing and Risk Assessment Branch, Safety Engineering Department CANDU Operations, AECL (February 1991–August 30, 1991).
+ Manager Reactor Physics Branch, Safety Engineering Department, CANDU Operations, AECL (June 1987–February 1991).
+ Liaison Officer, AECL CANDU Operations (June 1985–June 1987). This was a staff position with the responsibility to:

- ensure appropriate coordination of the R&D program at AECL Research Company with the needs of the power reactor design program at CANDU Operations.
- develop enhanced communications between technical staff at all AECL sites.
- to ensure human resources are effectively deployed to meet opportunities arising for AECL as a whole.

The work involved:

- monitoring of inter-site work and acting as an ombudsman on inter-site relations.
- establishing and keeping active a number of inter-site technical committees (served as chairman of two committees and a member of two others).
- spending significant time at CRNL and WNRE to maintain strong relationships with key staff.
- working closely with the Advanced CANDU group at CRNL, etc.

Previous Experience

- Operations Manager, Safety Engineering Department, CANDU Operations (January 1985–June 1985). Duties included:
  - Assist department manager in work planning, scheduling, and administrative activities for the Safety Engineering Department.
  - Provide consultations on technical issues related to reactor physics, fuel, and reactor low-power commissioning, as required.
- Manager, Physics Department, CANDU Operations (1979 to 1985).

- Manager of group responsible for reactor physics analysis, reactor shielding analysis, and reactor fuel design and analysis (for latter three years) associated with CANDU design.

- Reactor physics responsibility included supervision of low power commissioning of CANDU reactors, especially the 600-megawatt series (supervised a group of thirty-one professionals, six technologists, and three clerical staff, organized in two reactor physics branches and a fuel branch).

• Manager, Reactor Physics Branch, CANDU Operations (1967–1979).

- Responsible for reactor physics analysis associated with the design of Ontario Hydro CANDU reactors (Pickering and Bruce), including work related to planning and executions of low-power commissioning of these reactors. The scope of work in the branch included the following:

  ◊ Establishing reactor core design parameters.

  ◊ Defining the positions and performance characteristics of all reactivity control devices and neutron flux detectors.

  ◊ Development of fuel management strategies and calculating the fuel consumption rate expected in the reactor.

  ◊ Preparation of the Reactor Physics Design Manual for each reactor project and contributing sections to the safety analysis reports related to reactor neutronic characteristics.

  ◊ Pre-simulation of low-power physics tests for commissioning, assisting, or supervising execution of the tests and analysis of results.

◊ Supervised a group of fifteen professionals, three technologists, and one clerical staff.

- Analyst, Reactor Physics, CANDU Operations (1962–1967).

 - Analyst in the Physics and Analysis group responsible for analytical work for design of the Douglas Point and Pickering CANDU reactors. Worked as reactor physics specialist, later becoming section head of reactor physics. The work included:

 ◊ lattice and core physics calculations.

 ◊ development of computer programs for efficient simulations of neutronic behaviour of CANDU reactors (generally involved adapting/improving codes from CRNL or other research labs).

 ◊ studies of reactor performance characteristics for economic assessments.

- Analyst, Reactor Physics, NRU Operations Branch, CRNL (1957–1962).

 - Reactor physics analyst in the NRU Operations Physics Office, later serving as head of the reactor physics section. The work included:

 ◊ Recommending fuel management strategies and calculations.

 ◊ Predicting reactivity variations during reactor fuel burnup and power transients.

 ◊ Assisting researchers in design of in-core experimental programs.

 ◊ Producing a new fuel design in which natural uranium fuel is replaced with highly enriched U-A1 fuel.

Appendix

Some Special Tasks at AECL

+ Served on one of the internal audit teams performing the AECL comprehensive audit.

+ Coordinated the presentation of the Nuclear Fuel Cycle Bid for Yugoslavia with AECL Research Company in 1985–86.

+ Coordinated preparation of a detailed study report on use of enriched fuel cycles in an existing CANDU reactor for EPDC, Japan (in cooperation with CRNL) in 1984–85.

+ Reviewed the status of the technology of producing heavy water by isotope enrichment using lasers and produced a Layman's Overview report in 1986–87.

+ Assisted Marketing with the wording of fuel burnup warranties offered in reactor bids and in negotiations with clients in Korea, Argentina, Mexico, and Turkey.

Publications (Internal)

+ *Heavy Water Production by Laser Isotope Separation: A Layman's Overview*, by A. A. Pasanen, Adv CANDU-6. February 6, 1987.

+ *Physics Calculations for RAPP Core Design*, by A. A. Pasanen, TDSI-88, August 1971.

+ *The ABC's of Nuclear Reactor Kinetics*, by A. A. Pasanen, PP-7, October 1969.

+ *Feasibility of Using Large CANDU-like Power Reactors for Total or Partial Peak Load Operations*, by A. A. Pasanen, TDSI-52, May 1964.

+ *Equilibrium and Transient Reactivity Effects in CANDU-type Power Reactors Due to the Hold-up of Pu239 in Np239 and Sm149 in Pm149*, by A. A. Pasanen, TDSI-51, March 1964.

Publications (External)

+ *Fundamentals of CANDU Reactor Nuclear Design*, by A. A. Pasanen, IAEA-SMR 68/2, June 1982. A series of lectures given at the Trieste Institute for Theoretical Physics as part of a course on Operational Physics of Power Reactors.
+ Lectures on nuclear design and fuel management published in *CANDU Reactors: Lectures Presented to the International Atomic Energy Agency*, WNRE-521, October 12–16, 1981. Compiled by C.W. Zarecki.
+ *The Physics of CANDU On-Power Fueling: From Design Objective to Pickering Demonstration*, by A. A. Pasanen, IAEA SM 178/13, 1974.

Experience with the low-power commissioning of CANDU reactors as follows:

+ Participated in the Phase B part of the commissioning program of eleven CANDU reactors. Initial approach-to-critical and the tests to verify the physics characteristics of control and safety systems were as expected from the design analysis. Responsibilities included:
  - preparation of procedures together with utility staff.
  - analysis of results.
  - on-site as supervisor in three cases, consultant to utilities in two cases, and observer in two cases.